Teaching and Aging

Chandra M. N. Mehrotra, *Editor*

NEW DIRECTIONS FOR TEACHING AND LEARNING

KENNETH E. EBLE, *Editor-in-Chief*

Number 19, September 1984

Paperback sourcebooks in
The Jossey-Bass Higher Education Series

Jossey-Bass Inc., Publishers
San Francisco • Washington • London

Chandra M. N. Mehrotra (Ed.).
Teaching and Aging.
New Directions for Teaching and Learning, no. 19.
San Francisco: Jossey-Bass, 1984.

New Directions for Teaching and Learning Series
Kenneth E. Eble, *Editor-in-Chief*

New Directions for Teaching and Learning is published quarterly
by Jossey-Bass Inc., Publishers. Subscriptions, single-issue
orders, change of address notices, undelivered copies, and other
correspondence should be sent to Subscriptions, Jossey-Bass Inc.,
Publishers, 433 California Street, San Francisco, California 94104.

Editorial correspondence should be sent to the Editor-in-Chief,
Kenneth E. Eble, Department of English, University of Utah,
Salt Lake City, Utah 84112.

Library of Congress Catalogue Card Number LC 83-82746
International Standard Serial Number ISSN 0271-0633
International Standard Book Number ISBN 87589-792-4

Cover art by Willi Baum
Manufactured in the United States of America

Ordering Information

The paperback sourcebooks listed below are published quarterly and can be ordered either by subscription or single-copy.

Subscriptions cost $35.00 per year for institutions, agencies, and libraries. Individuals can subscribe at the special rate of $25.00 per year *if payment is by personal check.* (Note that the full rate of $35.00 applies if payment is by institutional check, even if the subscription is designated for an individual.) Standing orders are accepted. Subscriptions normally begin with the first of the four sourcebooks in the current publication year of the series. When ordering, please indicate if you prefer your subscription to begin with the first issue of the *coming* year.

Single copies are available at $8.95 when payment accompanies order, and *all single-copy orders under $25.00 must include payment.* (California, New Jersey, New York, and Washington, D.C., residents please include appropriate sales tax.) For billed orders, cost per copy is $8.95 plus postage and handling. (Prices subject to change without notice.)

Bulk orders (ten or more copies) of any individual sourcebook are available at the following discounted prices: 10–49 copies, $8.05 each; 50–100 copies, $7.15 each; over 100 copies, *inquire.* Sales tax and postage and handling charges apply as for single copy orders.

To ensure correct and prompt delivery, all orders must give either the *name of an individual* or an *official purchase order number.* Please submit your order as follows:

Subscriptions: specify series and year subscription is to begin.
Single Copies: specify sourcebook code (such as, TL8) and first two words of title.

Mail orders for United States and Possessions, Latin America, Canada, Japan, Australia, and New Zealand to:
    Jossey-Bass Inc., Publishers
    433 California Street
    San Francisco, California 94104

Mail orders for all other parts of the world to:
    Jossey-Bass Limited
    28 Banner Street
    London EC1Y 8QE

New Directions for Teaching and Learning Series
Kenneth E. Eble, *Editor-in-Chief*

Contents

Institutional concerns and faculty needs are reviewed, the characteristics of senior faculty are examined, and some approaches for extending the working life of these faculty members are explored.

Editor's Notes

This is the age of aging. Profound demographic shifts are pushing the average age of the population upward, and because of lower birthrates and longer life expectancy, this trend is likely to continue. The aging of the population creates new problems in every aspect of society, including the world of work: Both employers and employees must make major adjustments to deal with the transition from a younger labor force to an older one. These problems are especially acute in the case of colleges and universities.

What is so different about the situation in institutions of higher education as compared to other work settings? First, college professors are a highly select group of professionals in terms of their verbal abilities (their vocabulary, comprehension, information, writing abilities, and so on). Most of the work that they do depends on these abilities, which do not show significant decline until after the age of seventy. Thus, a large percentage of faculty members continue to contribute beyond the normal age of retirement. Second, due to the tenure system and to relatively little movement from academia into other kinds of work, colleges and universities have a low turnover rate. Third, institutions of higher education currently are experiencing a limited or no-growth situation. Finally, in view of the rapid development and advances occurring in all fields of study, these institutions must bring in recent Ph.D.s in order to maintain an adequate inflow of new ideas and skills. Thus, on the one hand, we have a large number of faculty in their forties and fifties who want to continue working until they are at least seventy, and, on the other hand, we have a no-growth situation that makes it difficult to infuse new blood into institutions of higher education. This creates problems for which innovative policies and programs need to be developed.

This sourcebook has been prepared to define these problems and challenges, to examine the relevant theories of adult development, and to explore innovative practices that can be beneficial to the institutions as well as to the members of the faculty.

In Chapter One, Linda K. George and Idee Winfield-Laird begin discussion of various issues related to aging faculty by presenting the age structure of the college and university faculty in the United States. They discuss the implications of the current age distribution in

1

terms of the cost of higher education, the reduction in administrative flexibility, the inflow of new ideas and skills, the effects on minorities and women, and the viability of academic careers. The chapter concludes with an exploration of possible interventions that can be used to alter the age structure of college faculty.

In Chapter Two, Charles S. Claxton and Patricia H. Murrell briefly discuss theories by Erik Erikson and Jane Loevinger and suggest how they relate to faculty at different points in their careers. The authors then apply these theories to several key areas of administrative practice and discuss their implications for college and university administrators.

Since professors change in important ways as they progress through their careers, it is essential to take into consideration their varying characteristics in designing professional development programs. In Chapter Three, Roger G. Baldwin discusses these faculty needs at different points in the academic career and suggests programs that would enable the institutions to meet the development needs of both mid-career and seasoned professors.

In Chapter Four, Janet H. Lawrence distinguishes between changes that are age-related and those that are cohort-related. She presents the argument that differences in philosophy and in teaching interests among professors, which are presently attributed to the aging process, may be due to the period during which they were socialized for their professional roles and to the type of educational experiences they had as students.

In Chapter Five, Betty Jane Myers and Richard E. Pearson report the findings of a study that they conducted to examine the feelings about retirement of a group of professors and administrators who were within five years of retiring. They describe the participants' views of the retirement transition in terms of perceived opportunities and assets, anticipated losses, valued activities, and significant contexts.

What can be done to enable retired professors to maintain a curious, active mind? This is a concern expressed often by academics anticipating retirement. One innovative program designed to meet these needs is presented in Chapter Six. Leo L. Nussbaum describes in some detail how the Academy of Senior Professionals at Eckerd College provides continued enrichment and stimulation to its members.

In the concluding chapter, I summarize the various problems, arguments, and viewpoints presented throughout this volume and suggest some programs and approaches that may be helpful to institutions as well as to their faculty.

The key issue that permeates the volume is this: How can we best utilize the available faculty of all ages in providing quality education in our colleges and universities? If this sourcebook promotes further discussion and research on this question and provides some impetus for initiating new programs, it will have achieved its purpose.

Chandra M. N. Mehrotra
Editor

Chandra M. N. Mehrotra is professor of psychology and associate dean for graduate studies at the College of St. Scholastica. His research and intellectual interests include the education and employment of older adults.

The aging of the academic labor force poses potentially serious problems for the quality of academic instruction and research and for the viability of academic careers.

Implications of an Aging Faculty for the Quality of Higher Education and Academic Careers

Linda K. George
Idee Winfield-Laird

One need spend very little time on a college or university campus today to recognize that occupational blockage, decreasing resources, and the viability of academic careers are salient issues. Graduate students worry about their employment prospects. Junior faculty worry about their tenure prospects. Senior faculty worry about declining enrollments, loss of faculty slots, and the possibility of retrenchment—with the latter threatening the jobs of even tenured faculty members. All of these concerns are valid; these are, indeed, tough times in academia.

Although concerns about the viability of academic careers and the quality of higher education are widespread, the relationship between such concerns and the aging of American college and university faculty has received relatively little attention. Clearly, the problems and issues facing higher education have many causes and multiple implications; the aging of college and university faculty is only one relevant issue, but it is an important one. This chapter examines three aspects of this

C. M. N. Mehrotra (Ed.). *Teaching and Aging.* New Directions for Teaching and Learning, no. 19. San Francisco: Jossey-Bass, September 1984.

5

issue: (1) the reasons for the aging of faculty in higher education, (2) the potential implications of an aging faculty for the quality of both higher education and academic careers, and (3) possible institutional responses to an aging faculty.

We must preface the examination of these issues with an explicit caveat. Because the aging of college and university faculty (henceforth referred to simply as college faculty) has received very little attention, relevant data are scant in volume and frequently problematic in nature. Available data are not comprehensive (for example, several academic disciplines are not included in the major data sources), are collected on an infrequent basis, and were collected for purposes other than the examination of the aging of college faculty. Consequently, the issues discussed in this chapter are examined in the context of fewer and less adequate data than are desirable. In spite of this, there are sufficient data to identify relevant trends and their implications.

The Aging of College Faculty

What is the evidence that college faculties are aging? How rapidly are college faculties aging? How widespread is this pattern? The answers to these questions are critical to setting the stage for future discussion. Although the data are slimmer in number and scope than we would like, these questions can be answered. In 1968–69, the median age of college faculty members was thirty-nine (Bayer, 1970); in 1972–73, the median age of college faculty members was forty (Corwin and Knepper, 1978); and by 1978–79, the median age of college faculty was forty-five (National Science Foundation, 1981a). Indeed, researchers predict that the median age of college faculty will continue to rise until about the end of the century (Cartter, 1976; Corwin and Knepper, 1978).

Current Age Distribution Statistics. There are two primary reasons that the median age of college faculty is expected to continue to increase. First, higher education is expected to remain a limited or no-growth industry for the foreseeable future (the factors leading to this situation are described later in this chapter). Second, the majority of college faculty members are middle-aged; consequently, the academic labor market is not expected to be substantially affected by out-migration due to retirement for fifteen to thirty more years. Table 1 presents the age distribution of doctoral scientists and engineers employed in American educational institutions in 1977. As the table indicates, the significant bulge of faculty members is in the middle of the distribution:

Table 1. Age Distribution of Doctoral Scientists and Engineers Employed in Educational Institutions: 1977

Age	Number	Percent
Under 30	5,423	3.3
30–34	30,126	18.5
35–39	37,225	22.8
40–44	25,832	15.8
45–49	22,178	13.6
50–54	17,901	11.0
55–59	13,112	8.0
60–54	7,697	4.7
65 and Older	3,421	2.1
No Report	186	.1
Total	163,101	100.00

Source: National Science Foundation, 1979.

More than half of the science and engineering faculty are age thirty-five to forty-nine. Consequently, even if faculty are replaced at a level equal to retirements, the age structure of the college faculty will not alter appreciably in the near future.

The scope of Table 1 merits brief comment. As the title of the table indicates, the data are restricted to engineering and science faculty (the latter includes the social sciences as well as the physical and life sciences). The National Science Foundation (NSF) carefully monitors manpower need and utilization in science and engineering and regularly issues detailed reports about the number and characteristics of scientists and engineers in the United States. These reports are the primary data sources available for the study of college faculty. Reliance upon NSF data obviously results in neglect of many relevant disciplines (for example, the humanities, health-related fields, and law). Unquestionably, then, the patterns described are based on a biased sample of academic disciplines. This situation reiterates the need for data that are broader in scope. For the present, we have no choice but to examine the age structure of college faculty on the basis of available data, but we must use appropriate caution and qualifications in generalizing from our findings.

Thus far, discussion of the aging of college faculty has focused directly on the chronological age of faculty members. In higher education, the chronological age structure of the labor force is compounded by two indicators of career age: academic rank and tenure status. In 1975, more than half of the academic labor force held the rank of associate or full professor (American Association of University Professors, 1976). The chronological age of the academic labor force has increased since 1975; consequently, the proportion of senior faculty members undoubtedly has increased also. The proportion of college faculty who are tenured also has increased over the past ten years. In 1968–69, about 47 percent of academic faculty were tenured (Bayer, 1970); by 1978–79, 66 percent of college faculty members were tenured (National Science Foundation, 1981b). Thus, whether one examines chronological age or career age, college faculty clearly are aging.

Although the aging of college faculty is a general pattern, there is considerable evidence that the extent and rate of aging varies across academic disciplines. Table 2 provides the median ages of American doctoral scientists and engineers in 1978–79, by academic department.

Table 2. Median Age of U.S. Science and Engineering Faculty by Department: 1978-79

Department	Median Age
Engineering:	
Aeronautical	47
Chemical	45
Civil	45
Electrical	48
Mechanical	48
Other Engineering	48
Environmental Science	41
Life Sciences:	
Agricultural Sciences	48
Biological Sciences	46
Computer Science	40
Mathematics	41
Physical Sciences:	
Chemistry	44
Physics	44
Astronomy	45
Other Physical Sciences	46
Psychology	45
Social Sciences:	
Economics	45
Political Science	43
Sociology	42
Other Social Sciences	42

Source: National Science Foundation, 1981a.

The medians range from forty to forty-eight. The "younger" disciplines include computer science, mathematics, and environmental sciences. The "oldest" faculties are found in electrical engineering, mechanical engineering, and agricultural sciences. Again, detailed data are restricted to science and engineering faculty. Some investigators, however, suggest that faculty in the humanities and in other liberal arts disciplines that are not monitored by the NSF are as old or even older (in terms of median age) than science and engineering faculty (Bayer, 1973; Cartter, 1976). Disciplinary differences in the age structures of faculty reflect two primary factors: (1) temporal fluctuations in the demand for college graduates in particular fields and (2) patterns of out-migration by mid-level and senior faculty. The greater the demand for graduates and the greater the out-migration of established faculty, the more junior faculty to be hired and the younger the age structure of the discipline.

Higher Education as a No-Growth Industry. As noted earlier, the major reason for the aging of college faculty is that higher education is a limited or no-growth industry. We turn now to a discussion of the major reasons for the stabilization and possible decline in the size of the academic marketplace. Where appropriate and possible on the basis of available data, we distinguish between undergraduate and graduate education.

The most important single factor responsible for the lack of growth in higher education is the stabilization and, more recently, the actual decrease in college enrollments. The primary cause of declining enrollments is demographic. Dramatic increases in birthrates after World War II resulted in a tremendously expanded academic labor market during the 1960s and early 1970s. Indeed, at that time, academic institutions were hard pressed to meet the demand for higher education. The baby boom generation has reached ages twenty-six to thirty-six, and its members have largely completed their educational attainments. Birthrates have decreased significantly since the late 1950s; as a consequence, there are simply fewer persons in the college-age population. In 1973, for example, there were 4,030,000 eighteen-year-olds in the United States; ten years later there are about 3,900,000. The number of college-age persons is expected to continue to decline until at least 1990, when there will be a projected 3,437,000 eighteen-year-olds (Cartter, 1976), leading demographers to predict concomitant declines in college enrollments. Indeed, some colleges already are experiencing at least slight declines in full-time enrollments. Early returns indicate that both undergraduate and graduate programs are suffering declining enrollments, but the largest decreases are in graduate programs.

Although lower birthrates are the major cause of declining college enrollments, other factors exacerbate the situation. During the 1960s and early 1970s, college enrollments increased both because of the *larger size* of the college-age population and because a *larger proportion* of that population enrolled in higher education. During this period, increased proportions of college-age youth found postsecondary education an attractive and possible goal. The increased availability of financial aid, an expanding labor market for college graduates, and a prosperous economy combined to increase the proportion of the potential pool of college students who enrolled in higher education. At the same time, graduate programs expanded rapidly (in part precisely because of the increased enrollments in undergraduate programs), thus generating a demand for new faculty. It was also during this period that increased numbers of minority students were recruited for undergraduate programs. Similarly, the numbers of both women and minorities entering graduate school increased dramatically in relative terms, although their absolute numbers continued to lag significantly behind those for white males.

The proportion of college-age youth enrolling in college now appears to have peaked and will either level off or, more probably, decline. Certainly, the major factors attracting new types of students to college campuses during the 1960s and early 1970s are no longer operative. Public programs providing financial aid to college students have been severely reduced. More importantly, the economy has weakened and the economic value of a college degree has been called into serious doubt.

Public investments in research and development also have affected the growth rate of academic institutions. During the last ten years, federal investments in research and development have leveled off and, in many fields, have experienced absolute declines (National Science Foundation, 1980a). This has had three primary consequences for the academic labor force: First, decreased research and development funding has limited the number of jobs available to college graduates — at least those graduating in science and engineering. As a result, there is less demand for college graduates and enrollments are declining. This pattern has been especially true for doctoral graduates and graduate school enrollments. Second, out-migration of college faculty to research positions in the public and private sectors has been reduced. Third, institutions of higher education have traditionally used research funds to increase their faculties. The restriction of research and development funds has decreased the inflow of research-based faculty to academic institutions, especially entry-level Ph.D.s.

Student-Faculty Ratios and Tenure Decisions. Policy decisions by academic institutions also have contributed to the uneven age structure of college faculty. During the 1965–1974 decade, student-faculty ratios decreased significantly (U.S. Office of Education, 1975). These reductions in student-faculty ratios undoubtedly were beneficial for the quality of higher education; however, they also contributed to rapid expansion of academic faculties in the late 1960s and early 1970s. Faculty members hired during that time are now part of the middle-aged bulge of faculty members who are sufficiently senior to be tenured but who also are fifteen to thirty years from the normal retirement age. Further reductions in student-faculty ratios are unlikely. Consequently, this former impetus to faculty growth has become inoperative.

Although firm data are scanty, it also appears that, during the past decade, institutions of higher learning have become less likely to grant tenure to junior faculty. It is common knowledge that the criteria for tenure have become more stringent (in a benevolent mood, some senior faculty members will admit that they would not have received tenure under current standards). Many institutions also have reduced the number of new faculty given "tenure-track" appointments. These administrative policies undoubtedly are responses to a limited or no-growth situation. At the same time, however, such policies exacerbate the aging of the college faculty.

Federal Legislation and Out-Migration. Recent changes in federal legislation also may accelerate the trend toward an aging college faculty. In 1978, Congress passed amendments to the Age Discrimination in Employment Act (ADEA), extending the age of mandatory retirement to seventy for most industries, including higher education. The ADEA amendments did not take affect until 1982, so it still is too early to measure their impact. Many argue that their impact will be small because (1) many institutions already have a mandatory retirement age of seventy and (2) most college faculty are covered by both private and public pensions, permitting departure from the labor force prior to the mandatory retirement age if that is what the individual desires. Nonetheless, other evidence suggests that college professors usually work as long as possible (Fillenbaum and Maddox, 1974; Rowe, 1972). Consequently, the ADEA amendments may contribute to the aging of college faculty in the future.

Another contributing factor is that higher education traditionally has had very low rates of out-migration compared to other industries. Moreover, older workers in all industries are less likely than younger workers to change jobs or occupations voluntarily — and this pattern holds true for college faculty. The tenure system makes involuntary out-migration of older workers especially unlikely in the academic marketplace. Available data suggest that, on average, 7.7 percent of the academic labor force changes jobs each year (Corwin and Knepper, 1978). Reflecting the decreased mobility of older workers, however, the turnover rate of full-time tenured faculty is about 4.2 percent. About half of the turnover of full-time tenured faculty is due to retirement and about half is due to job changes (both within academia and across employment sectors). Current market conditions provide little reason to expect rates of out-migration to increase in the near future. As we mentioned previously, at least some older faculty members probably will extend their working years to age seventy, and decreases in research and development funding have restricted the opportunity structure for sector changes in employment during the preretirement years. Given the current situation, in which academic institutions are producing more Ph.D.s than can be employed in the fields for which they have trained (National Science Foundation, 1980b), the traditionally low rate of out-migration and turnover among college faculty may decrease even further in the future.

Slow Response to Change. A final factor that is relevant to the aging of college faculty merits brief attention: the lag between changes in external conditions and the appropriate responses of institutions of higher education. It is tempting to conclude that the organization of higher education has simply failed to react effectively to changes in external conditions. We would agree that increased emphasis can and should be placed on the more predictable factors affecting the growth or retrenchment of the academic marketplace (such as demographic projections of the size of the college-age population). Beyond this, however, opportunities for rational long-term planning may be limited. It is very difficult to predict changes in many of the factors affecting academic growth (such as the cycles of prosperity and recession in the larger economy or the future demand for college graduates in specific disciplines).

Furthermore, academic institutions do respond to changing external circumstances — they simply require a considerable amount of time to do so. For example, the size of the academic labor force increased rapidly in response to the burgeoning enrollments of the 1960s. Unfortunately, given the length of time needed to train the increased number of faculty, the baby boom generation completed their education at about the same time that academic institutions were best equipped to handle the increased enrollment. Such lags have contributed to the current age structure of college faculties.

In summary, a number of demographic, social, and administrative factors have combined to result in a limited or even no-growth academic labor force, accompanied by an aging college faculty. Moreover, it appears that the conditions restricting academic growth will persist for the near future and that the age of American college faculty will increase during the same period. How significant is this state of affairs? What are the implications of an aging college faculty? We turn now to a consideration of such issues.

The Implications of an Aging College Faculty

The implications of aging faculty for academic institutions are a matter of conjecture (albeit informed conjecture) rather than fact. There are no systematic data that definitively document the consequences of an aging academic labor force. Nonetheless, strong arguments and supporting data suggest that the aging of the college faculty has implications that are, at minimum, consequential and that may be critical for the quality of higher education in the United States. In this section, we examine five aspects of the nature and quality of higher education that may be affected by an aging faculty.

The Cost of Higher Education. An aging and thus tenured and highly ranked faculty has obvious implications for the cost of higher education. In terms of average compensation in 1975–76, for example, an associate professor cost $3,538 more than an assistant professor and a full professor cost $6,551 more than an associate professor (American Association of University Professors, 1976). Assistant professors, who represent relative bargains in cost, are suffering reductions in employment because of the aging and tenured senior faculty. Some would argue that a more senior faculty will be associated with higher-quality instruction; many more would argue against such a claim. At any rate, the cost of instruction inevitably increases when the labor force is older, tenured, and of higher academic rank.

Reduction in Administrative Flexibility. There is general agreement that colleges and universities should be intellectually broad-based and should include a wide range of disciplines. Beyond this, however, there is no general consensus regarding the optimum distributions of faculty members and other resources across disciplines (Furniss, 1973). We do know, however, that societal demands for individuals with particular kinds of training change over time and that there is a lagged but related change in student interest in various kinds of academic training (Freeman, 1971). The capacity of an institution to adapt its programs to changing educational and career interests of students depends to a substantial degree on administrative flexibility in rearranging and changing the mix of faculty (the distribution of faculty across disciplines). Such flexibility is decreased by an aging, highly tenured faculty.

Adequate Inflow of New Ideas and Skills. The academic environment has a continuing need for new ideas, skills, insights, and methodologies. Moreover, the current rate at which new knowledge and techniques are generated is very high. It is theoretically possible for the members of an aging faculty to remain current with regard to new scholarship and scientific advances. The sabbatical leave, for example, is justified in large part by the expectation of continuing education, and to some extent, the retooling of faculty members.

In practical terms, however, the assurance of a steady inflow of recently trained junior faculty is probably a preferred strategy for ensuring an adequate inflow of new ideas, techniques, and skills into academic institutions. The evidence concerning the relationship between career age and scholarly productivity is complex and, to some extent, contradictory (Allison and Stewart, 1974; Bayer and Dutton, 1975; Clemente, 1973; Zuckerman and Merton, 1972). Space limitations preclude an extensive review of this body of research. However, there is reason to believe that (1) the hypothesis that increased career age is associated with decreased productivity merits serious consideration and (2) the relationship between career age and productivity varies considerably by discipline. Concern about the implications of an aging faculty for the inflow of new knowledge and optimum scientific productivity appears legitimate.

Effects on Minorities and Women. Minorities and women, who first began to realize significant increases in graduate training during the late 1960s and early 1970s, are especially affected by the aging of the academic labor force. The situation of limited or no growth in the academic marketplace affects female and minority scholars adversely in terms of both initial entry and in their promotion from junior ranks. That is, in a stable or declining labor market, females and members of minority groups suffer, even with the amelioration of affirmative action programs, from variants of the well-known last hired–first fired principle. From the viewpoint of academic diversity, this pattern also is problematic. It is ironic that the same boom in academic enrollments that prepared increased numbers of women and minority group members for the academic marketplace also is responsible, to a significant degree, for the restricted employment opportunities now open to women and minorities.

The Viability of Academic Careers. Substantial investment of resources is involved in preparation for an academic career. Moreover, although we know of no research that clearly demonstrates a positive association between orderliness of one's career and productivity, intuitively we would expect such an association. That is, if a substantial majority of persons trained for academic careers in teaching and research are forced, at the beginning of their careers, to take jobs outside academic institutions—jobs in academic settings with uncertain career lines or jobs totally outside the fields in which they were trained—we would expect the quality of the pool of persons available for academic employment in future years to suffer. In fact, there is currently sufficient evidence concerning declining enrollments in doctoral programs to elevate concern about this issue (National Science Foundation, 1980b). Information about the quality of the reduced pool of doctoral students is not available, but it seems reasonable to speculate that the quality of the pool has declined somewhat. Ultimately, this may be the most consequential implication of an aging academic labor force. If the viability of academic careers is very low over a substantial period of time, the quality of the pool of persons seeking such careers eventually will be reduced—as will the quality of future teaching and research efforts in academic organizations.

In summary, the aging of college faculty has several potential negative implications for the quality of higher education both in the near and more distant futures. Evidence supporting a link between an aging faculty and decreased quality of instruction and research is admittedly weak because of little systematic study of the issues involved. Those who wish to await the availability of firmer evidence may consider the issues just described as hypotheses to be evaluated at a later time. We find the logic of the five issues, however, quite compelling. And, perhaps most impressive, we have not found a single discussion of the changing age structure of college faculty that views the pattern as anything less than cause for concern. Moreover, although we would not suggest that such findings are directly applicable to the academic marketplace, economists have documented declines in productivity and quality of output among other industries suffering limited or declining growth.

Intervening to Alter the Age Structure of College Faculty

In spite of limited data, the potentially negative implications of an aging academic work force have been treated seriously by both scientific observers and college administrators. Indeed, the potentially dysfunctional consequences of an aging college faculty have been taken so seriously that interventions designed to alter the age structure of college faculties have been proposed and, in a few cases, put into limited practice. In this section, we review six interventions that have been proposed as incentives for the out-migration of senior faculty from academic institutions. Two of the proposed interventions are designed to reduce academic commitments to senior faculty nearing retirement. The other four interventions have been proposed as methods of encouraging out-migration of middle-aged faculty who are still many years away from an acceptable retirement age. In addition to describing the six types of intervention, we will assess the degree to which each appears to respond effectively to the potential problems posed by an aging academic labor force.

Inducements to Encourage Early Retirement. In American society as a whole, rates of early retirement have increased dramatically over the past twenty years. Indeed, recent estimates suggest that 40 percent of the labor force retires before age sixty-five (Sheppard, 1976). Surveys of the preretirement population suggest that many more workers would retire before the usual retirement age if they could afford to do so (Harris and Associates, 1975). Given this societal trend, some observers believe that financial incentives could be used to increase significantly the out-migration of older faculty members who are at or near the usual retirement age. These observers are convinced that inducements for early retirement could be effective in spite of the fact that some research previously cited indicates that most professors work as long as they are permitted to and continue professional activity after retirement.

There have been experiments with early retirement programs at selected institutions. Such programs have achieved varying degrees of success as measured by the net increase in retirements and the satisfaction of the early retirees (Jenny, 1974; Kell and Patton, 1978; Patton, 1977). The specific inducements used to encourage early retirements vary from program to program, but they include one-time cash payments, continuing supplements, continuation of pension contributions, continuation of life and medical insurance, and continuation of other fringe benefits (such as reduced tuition for children). Some programs use a single incentive; others use combinations of inducements.

The policies regarding eligibility for early retirement are an important aspect of the probable effectiveness of such programs. In some programs, eligibility is universal (that is, all faculty of a certain age or meeting a length-of-service requirement are eligible). In other programs, eligibility is selective and incentives for early retirement are offered only to those faculty members that the institution wishes to encourage to retire. Both models of eligibility have advantages and disadvantages. Universal eligibility probably generates the highest amount of net out-migration, but it increases the risk that the most productive eligible faculty members will opt for early retirement at that institution and obtain employment elsewhere—thus reducing the overall quality of the faculty. Selective eligibility provides administrative flexibility permitting quality control, but administrators may be unwilling to use it and faculty members—both those to whom it is offered and those to whom it is denied—may object to its use.

Phased Retirement or Part-Time Employment. A majority of the population age sixty and older—both those retired and those in the labor force—report that they would prefer part-time work to either full-time work or to complete retirement (Harris and Associates, 1975). Many who wish to retire completely at some point also would like first to reduce their work commitment to part-time employment. This broad social trend also might be attractive to college faculty. Offered at the end of the career line, part-time work or gradual retirement would typically coincide with reduced income needs on the part of the faculty member (for example, children may no longer be financially dependent). Such options also might ease the social and psychological aspects of the retirement transition. Such incentives might be particularly attractive to those professors who cannot obtain alternate employment and those who do not wish to invest in retraining for alternate employment because they are close to the usual retirement age.

From the point of view of the academic institution, of course, reductions in the duties assigned to senior faculty would be a method of reducing the institution's financial commitments to relatively expensive members of the faculty. Again, eligibility for part-time employment and gradual retirement could be either universal or selective. The advantages and disadvantages of the two eligibility models are the same as those described in the preceding section.

An Across-the-Board Reduction in Relative Salaries. A major principle of economic theory is the proposition that a reduction in wages, relative to those paid in competing industries, will lead to increased out-migration of workers. Thus, if administrators implemented salary raises such that college faculty gain less than their counterparts in government or private industry, increased out-migration of college faculty should be observed. The amount of increased out-migration would be determined by the magnitude of the salary reductions and by the opportunity structure outside academic institutions (such as the relative salaries and number of openings at alternate places of employment). In the case of academic fields, there would be large disciplinary differences in opportunities for alternate employment (for example, engineers can move to private industry quite easily while historians cannot).

There seem to be several problems that would result from the application of this strategy. First, a decline in the wage structure may not alter the age structure of college faculty. Reductions in relative wages should increase out-migration by faculty of all ages, as well as discourage new Ph.D.s from seeking employment in the academic sector. Moreover, a great deal of evidence suggests that older workers will find it more difficult to move than younger workers. Consequently, this strategy could exacerbate rather than help the trend toward an aging faculty.

Second, because of the disciplinary differences in alternate opportunity structures, the increase in out-migration would be expected to vary widely across disciplines. Because different disciplines are "aging" at different rates, these disciplinary differences in increased out-migration might result in more problematic age structures for some academic fields.

Third, and most important, implementation of this strategy might have very negative consequences for the quality of college faculty. The best faculty would be the most attractive to alternate employment sectors. Thus, this strategy would run the risk that the high-quality faculty would be able to move and would do so while the lower-quality faculty members would be unable to obtain alternate employment and would stay in their academic institutions. The same process might affect the quality of new Ph.D.s willing to work in the academic labor force. The new entrants with the best potential would be very attractive to business or government and might choose to forgo academic employment in favor of the higher salaries of other employment sectors. Thus, the quality of college faculties might be eroded or lessened by lower relative salaries for the academic marketplace.

Finally, and obviously, college faculties could be expected to be very unhappy with the application of this strategy.

We are not aware of any deliberate policy decisions by administrators to implement across-the-board reductions in relative salaries for the purpose of encouraging the out-migration of college faculty. Some observers argue, however, that we have in fact been observing a type of natural experiment in this regard. For the past several years, academic salaries have been in a period of relative decline (American Association of University Professors, 1976). At this point, however, the impact of this decline upon out-migration of college faculty is not clear. In fact, the recent relative decline of faculty salaries probably will not prove to be a good test of its impact upon out-migration because this decline has occurred in the context of a generally weak economy, and many industries, including those that serve as alternate sources of employment for academic manpower, also have experienced relative salary declines. A true test of the theory behind this proposition would occur only when academic salaries experience sizable declines relative to alternate employment sectors.

Selective Application of Wage Reductions. Some authors argue that a selective application of wage reductions is preferable to an across-the-board reduction in relative faculty salaries. Using this strategy, administrators would reduce the relative salaries of nonproductive personnel or those faculty members whom the institution wanted to induce to leave (these reductions would be relative to the salaries of high-quality faculty and to average salaries in other employment sectors). The advantage of this strategy is that the burden of salary declines would be placed squarely upon the specific faculty members that the institutions most want to move. If such a policy was successful, it is argued, the institution could open slots for younger faculty members or decrease total faculty size without reducing the quality of the senior faculty. The actual impact of a program of selective wage reductions would depend upon the degree of salary cuts, the frequency of its use, and the criteria used in its application.

There is no question that the plan for selective wage reductions would, in theory, avoid some of the major problems identified for universal reductions in relative salaries. Most importantly, the selective application of wage reductions would be expected to prevent the out-migration of the highest-quality senior faculty. This strategy also would result in academic employment remaining attractive to the brightest and best of the potential new entrants. Selective wage reductions also could be implemented such that the needs of specific disciplines were taken into account and the age structure of the faculty was altered in desirable ways.

The greatest disadvantage of the selective wage reduction strategy is that it probably would be strongly opposed by faculty — and perhaps also by administrators. Selective application of wage incentives presumably operates in the current academic market. Although absolute reductions in salaries probably are exceedingly rare, raises in academic salaries often are assumed to be dependent upon productivity and general occupational performance. There are no firm data on this point; our impression, however, is that administrators often are reluctant to make hard decisions based on merit. In addition, greater numbers of academic institutions are moving to across-the-board, cost-of-living wage increases — sometimes in response to pressures from collective bargaining efforts of faculties. Thus, selective applications of relative wage reductions probably would face strong oppositions by both faculty and administrators.

A Decrease in Wage Differentials by Age and Rank. Traditionally, wage differences between faculty members of different ranks have been quite dramatic. As we noted earlier, in 1976 an associate professor earned, on average, $3,538 more than an assistant professor and a full professor earned $6,551 more than an associate professor. Some authors have suggested that a flattening of the age/rank earnings profile for college faculty (by decreasing differences in salary across ranks) might relieve some of the pressures that are producing an aging academic labor force. Using this strategy, administrators would be relieved of the need to make decisions about the application of selective wage reductions. Colleges also could retain their ability to attract high-quality new Ph.D.s for academic jobs because the incentive to out-migrate would fall on senior personnel.

Nonetheless, this strategy also has some problems and limitations. First, the less productive faculty with fewer opportunities for alternate employment might be more likely to stay in academic institutions, while the best and brightest senior faculty members might accept nonacademic employment at higher salaries. Thus, as with universal wage reductions, the quality of the senior faculty might suffer from the implementation of this strategy. Second, out-migration is more difficult for older workers in all industries because of increased worker reluctance to move and because alternate opportunity structures are more limited and less willing to hire older workers. Also, as we noted earlier, there are disciplinary differences in the ability to obtain employment outside the academic sector. Consequently, this strategy would place an unequal burden on senior members of some disciplines compared to the burden placed on senior members of other disciplines. Finally, one would expect strong opposition from senior faculty to this strategy.

It is interesting to note that as early as 1975 Cartter and McDowell reported that age/rank differentials in faculty salaries already had started to decline. If this is the case, the 1976 salary data presented above suggest that there is considerable room for even greater flattening of the age/rank salary profile. It is unclear whether this is a stable trend; if so, it still is too early to assess its impact.

Retraining for Career Change. The phrase *inducement to out-migration* implies that faculty members who are satisfied with their careers might be nudged into out-migration. We should not lose sight of the fact, however, that there may be some college faculty members who are in fact eager to change occupations and are simply waiting for an appropriate opportunity to out-migrate. Some of these professors may want to continue working in their current field, albeit in a different sector of the economy. Others, however, may want not only alternate employment but also alternate careers. There are no firm data concerning the number or ages of college faculty members who would like to change careers. A survey by the American Council on Education (Bayer, 1973), however, found that 13 percent of tenured faculty members expressed dissatisfaction with their jobs, reported that they would not pursue their current occupation if they "had it to do over," and would be interested in alternate careers.

Academic institutions are in an ideal position to offer career counseling, job market information, and retraining opportunities to their faculties. If such programs are to be effective, the retraining probably should be offered at little cost and in conjunction with reduced job responsibilities.

The greatest advantage of this strategy is that out-migration could be facilitated among precisely those faculty members who most want to move, thus reducing faculty-administration conflict. Age, rank, or length-of-service requirements could be used to govern access to the program and to ensure that the resulting out-migration occurs among the middle-aged and older faculty. An additional advantage of this strategy is that it would be useful to those persons from disciplines that face very limited opportunity structures outside the academic marketplace.

There are some potential disadvantages to this strategy also. Most important, it is unclear whether the quality of the senior faculty would be affected by the availability of retraining programs. That is, it is not clear whether high-quality faculty would be more or less likely than lower-quality faculty to take advantage of the retraining programs and eventually to migrate from academic careers. If there were strong utilization of such programs by the highest-quality senior faculty, such programs could have unfortunate consequences for the quality of academic research and instruction. In addition, such programs could be very expensive.

We are aware of a number of current programs designed to help younger Ph.D.s and junior faculty members retool for alternate careers, such as postdoctoral training programs for young Ph.D.s and programs designed to help junior faculty who are denied tenure to locate alternate employment. We are not aware of any retraining programs specifically designed to facilitate mid-career change among senior faculty. Of course, some dissatisfied senior faculty undoubtedly pursue mid-career change and obtain the prerequisite training without such programs.

These six strategies represent potential interventions that college administrators could implement in response to the pressures of an aging academic labor force. It is not clear that any of these strategies are likely to be broadly implemented by academic institutions. Indeed, it is more likely that administrators will not make deliberate efforts to alter the age structures of their faculties. Nonetheless, some of these strategies may occur anyway, simply as a response to general economic conditions and the external circumstances impinging upon the academic labor market. The relative decline in academic wages over the past decade is a case in point.

We will not express preferences for specific strategies designed to alter the age structure of college faculties; indeed, we will not even evaluate the desirability of deliberate attempts to alter the faculty age structure. But, before leaving the topic of interventions, we wish to reiterate and put into perspective some of the relevant issues.

One such issue is the question of where to intervene in the age structure of college faculty. Incentives for early retirement probably are more acceptable to the academic labor force than other interventions and are easiest to implement because such programs are relatively common in many industries and because there is a societal trend favoring early retirement. Given the age distribution of the U.S. college faculty, however, the net out-migration resulting from such programs will be quite small. The bulge of tenured faculty are ages thirty-five to fifty and thus are years away from an acceptable retirement age. The greatest out-migration would be realized by using interventions aimed at mid-career movement out of academic institutions. The interventions most likely to increase mid-career out-migration, however, probably would be less acceptable to both faculty and administrators.

The issue of universal versus selective eligibility for incentive programs also is difficult. The risk of universal applicability is that the best faculty members will be more likely to use the incentive programs thus posing a threat to the quality of the remaining academic faculty. Selective eligibility, in theory, could be used to ensure that high-quality faculty are encouraged to stay in academic institutions and that lower-quality faculty are encouraged to leave. The criteria for selective eligibility are troublesome, however, and increased resistance would be expected among both faculty and administrators. There simply is no easy answer to this quandary and thus far there are insufficient data to evaluate the degree to which universal versus selective criteria have significant effects upon faculty quality.

The issue of cost was largely ignored in discussions of the advantages and disadvantages of the six intervention strategies. In the absence of firm data, explicit cost comparisons are precluded. Certain conclusions can be suggested, however. Strategies that reduce academic salaries — either selectively or across the board — should realize savings to academic institutions and be attractive to administrators on at least those grounds. Retraining programs and early retirement programs, on the other hand, would involve considerable expense. Consequently, systematic demonstration and evaluation of the costs and benefits of such strategies probably would be required before substantial proliferation of such programs can be expected. Cost will be an important factor in the utilization of any of these interventions, and specific cost information about the cost of implementing and operating such programs is badly needed.

Although we previously noted that the chronological age structure of college faculties is compounded by rank and tenure, a few addditional comments about the implications of the latter are in order. It is commonly asserted, particularly by economists and administrators, that tenure (although useful for many other reasons) is dysfunctional for administrative flexibility and planning (Commission on Academic Tenure in Higher Education, 1973; Mann, 1973; Smith, 1973). Tenure, it is argued, makes academic planning problematic at best and irrational at worst. Proponents of this perspective argue that modifications of the faculty age structure while retaining faculty excellence, for example, would be rather easily implemented were it not for the career commitments posed by the tenure system. Although the tenure system undoubtedly does affect academic planning, we view many of these arguments as "straw men" that administrators use to shield themselves from being held accountable for developing effective responses to the problems facing higher education. In the interests of fairness, we add that faculty members also propagate myths concerning their inability to respond effectively to similar problems. Although available data are not conclusive, it appears that administrators often do not use the power available to them with regard to merit pay increases and allocation of other resources. Moreover, perhaps the most dysfunctional aspect of the tenure debate (or, more accurately, of the use of tenure as a scapegoat) is that it is one of several factors that discourages faculty members and administrators from working together to respond effectively to the problems posed by an aging academic labor force. This, as well as other problems facing higher education, will not be solved easily, but adversarial relationships between faculty and administrators only make effective responses less likely.

Finally, none of the possible interventions we examined was based on the intent to respond to an aging academic labor force by upgrading the knowledge and skills of an aging faculty. Some observers would prefer that interventions be used to retain academic quality with an aging faculty rather than to encourage out-migration of senior faculty. Of course, this is not necessarily an either/or situation—programs could be implemented that both upgrade the knowledge of some senior faculty and encourage the out-migration of others. Several of the chapters in this volume address the issue of faculty development at middle and later stages of the academic career line—and the prospects for such programs seem promising. We would add one qualification to an endorsement of faculty development programs as a response to an aging academic labor force, however. Such programs might help to alleviate concerns that an aging academic labor force will have negative consequences for the quality of academic research and instruction. In the absence of either significant growth or replacement of faculty in academic institutions, however, the ability to attract bright young adults to the academic enterprise will be severely limited. Thus, although faculty development programs may facilitate quality instruction, they cannot increase the viability of academic careers for younger adults.

Final Comments

This chapter has examined several aspects of aging college and university faculty: We have documented that the academic labor force is aging, examined the reasons for this trend, considered the potentially negative consequences of an aging college faculty, and described interventions that have been recommended to alter the trend toward an aging academic labor force. The topic of an aging college faculty is complicated by the lack of data and relevant research; thus, attempts to describe the implications of this trend and of strategies for responding effectively rest on a shaky foundation.

Because of this, one response to this chapter might be: "What if we ignore the aging of college faculty? These things tend to work themselves out if we just let them." A response of that kind cannot be dismissed summarily. And, in fact, there will be pressures toward self-correction in the academic labor market—even in the absence of intervention. Available projections suggest that the size of the college-age population will stabilize by the early 1990s and may even increase slightly in the following decade (Cartter, 1976). College enrollments should follow the same pattern. Federal agencies (National Science Foundation, 1980a) and political leaders reassure us that, although research and development funds will not experience dramatic increases, they too should stabilize at predictable patterns of modest growth. In another fifteen to thirty years, what is now a middle-aged bulge of faculty members will be retiring in droves, breaking the academic market-place wide open. Moreover, there is the inevitable lag between changing external conditions and institutional responses to those conditions. If academic institutions started now to respond to the pressures of an aging labor force, chances are that the results wouldn't be observed until about the time the issue had ceased to be relevant.

As this logic suggests, a case can be made for allowing nature to take its course. As we stated earlier, however, a strong case also can be made for attempting to respond effectively and actively to the problems posed by an aging academic labor force. Our intent has not been to advocate either position. We do believe, however, that the potential implications of an aging college faculty merit increased attention. More data, systematic research, and scholarly debate all should be brought to bear on the issue. If this demographic pattern is left to work itself out without intervention, we would prefer that this benevolent neglect be the result of informed consideration of the issues involved. Similarly, if intervention is used to respond to the pressures of an aging college faculty, this approach should be based on informed examination of relevant issues. Although the outcome of a scholarly examination of the implications of an aging academic labor force remains uncertain, such an examination clearly is warranted.

References

Allison, P. D., and Stewart, J. A. "Productivity Differences Among Scientists: Evidence for Accumulative Advantage." *American Sociological Review,* 1974, *39* (4), 596–606.

American Association of University Professors. *Nearly Keeping Up: Report of the Profession, 1975–76.* Washington, D.C.: American Association of University Professors, 1976.

Bayer, A. E. *College and University Faculty: A Statistical Description.* Washington, D.C.: American Council on Education, 1970.

Bayer, A. E. *Teaching Faculty in Academe: 1972–73.* Washington, D.C.: American Council on Education, 1973.

Bayer, A. E., and Dutton, J. E. "Career Age and Research-Professional Activities of Academic Scientists: Tests of Alternative Nonlinear Models and Their Implications for Higher Education Faculty Policies." Paper presented at the annual meeting of the American Educational Research Association, 1975.

Cartter, A. M. *Ph.D.s and the Academic Labor Market.* New York: McGraw-Hill, 1976.

Cartter, A. M., and McDowell, J. M. "Changing Employment Patterns and Faculty Demographics." In A. M. Cartter (Ed.), *Assuring Academic Progress Without Growth.* New Directions for Institutional Research, no. 6. San Francisco: Jossey-Bass, 1975.

Clemente, F. "Early Career Determinants of Research Productivity." *American Journal of Sociology,* 1973, *79* (3), 409–419.

Commission on Academic Tenure in Higher Education. W. R. Keast (Ed.). *Faculty Tenure: A Report and Recommendations.* San Francisco: Jossey-Bass, 1973.

Corwin, T. M., and Knepper, P. R. *Finance and Employment Implications of Raising the*

26

Mandatory Retirement Age for Faculty. Washington, D.C.: American Council on Education, 1978.

Fillenbaum, G., and Maddox, G. "Work After Retirement: An Investigation into Some Psychologically Relevant Variables." *The Gerontologist,* 1974, *14* (3), 418–424.

Freeman, R. B. *The Market for College-Trained Manpower.* Cambridge, Mass.: Harvard University Press, 1971.

Furniss, W. T. *Steady-State Staffing in Tenure-Granting Institutions and Related Papers.* Washington, D.C.: American Council on Education, 1973.

Harris, L., and Associates, Inc. *The Myth and Reality of Aging in America.* Washington, D.C.: National Council on Aging, 1975.

Jenny, H. H. *Early Retirement.* New York: Teachers Insurance and Annuity Association of America, 1974.

Kell, D., and Patton, C. V. "Reaction to Induced Early Retirement." *The Gerontologist,* 1978, *18* (2), 173–179.

Mann, W. R. "The Tenure Controversy." *The Education Digest,* 1973, *39* (1), 12–15.

National Science Foundation. *Characteristics of Doctoral Scientists and Engineers in the U.S.: 1977.* Washington, D.C.: U.S. Government Printing Office, 1979.

National Science Foundation. *Academic Science, 1972–77: R&D Funds, Scientists and Engineers, Graduate Enrollment and Support.* Washington, D.C.: U.S. Government Printing Office, 1980a.

National Science Foundation. *Employment Attributes of Recent Science and Engineering Graduates.* Washington, D.C.: U.S. Government Printing Office, 1980b.

National Science Foundation. *Activities of Science and Engineering Faculty in Universities and Four-Year Colleges: 1978–79.* Washington, D.C.: U.S. Government Printing Office, 1981a.

National Science Foundation. *Science Resources Studies Highlights: Tenure Practices in Universities and Four-Year Colleges Affect Faculty Turnover.* Washington, D.C.: U.S. Government Printing Office, 1981b.

Patton, C. V. "Early Retirement in Academia: Making the Decision." *The Gerontologist,* 1977, *17* (3), 347–354.

Rowe, A. R. "The Retirement of Academic Scientists." *Journal of Gerontology,* 1972, *27* (2), 113–118.

Sheppard, H. L. "Work and Retirement." In R. H. Binstock and E. Shanas (Eds.), *Handbook of Aging and the Social Sciences.* New York: Van Nostrand Reinhold, 1976.

Smith, B. L. (Ed.). *The Tenure Debate.* San Francisco: Jossey-Bass, 1973.

U.S. Office of Education. *Projections of Educational Statistics to 1982–83.* Washington, D.C.: U.S. Government Printing Office, 1975.

Zuckerman, H., and Merton, R. K. "Age and Aging, and Age Structure in Science." In M. W. Riley, M. Johnson, and A. Foner (Eds.), *Aging and Society: Volume III — A Sociology of Age Stratification.* New York: Russell Sage Foundation, 1972.

Linda K. George is associate professor in the Department of Psychiatry and senior fellow at the Center for the Study of Aging and Human Development at Duke University. Her research examines many of the social and social-psychological aspects of human aging.

Idee Winfield-Laird is a Ph.D. candidate in the Duke University Department of Sociology. Her dissertation focuses upon the relationship between organizational opportunity structures and career patterns.

Adult development research and theory illuminate significant
issues, concerns, and motivations of senior faculty members
and provide insight into sound administrative practices and
a positive institutional environment.

Developmental Theory as a Guide for Maintaining the Vitality of College Faculty

Charles S. Claxton
Patricia H. Murrell

Key administrators in today's higher education confront an entire complex of difficult issues. Of particular concern are the needs of senior faculty, whose numbers are increasing steadily, as George and Winfield-Laird have emphasized in their introductory pages to Chapter One. At present the majority of faculty are between thirty-five and forty-five years of age (Shulman, 1979). By the end of the present decade, 35 percent will be over age fifty-five, and by the year 2000 more than half of the faculty will be over fifty-five (Carnegie Council on Policy Studies in Higher Education, 1980).

The way to ensure that older faculty members remain creative and productive is to carry out personnel policies designed to provide a context in which people can grow and develop as they move through the life cycle. The purpose of this chapter, then, is to discuss a rationale, based on adult development theory, that can help administrators promote the continuing vitality of faculty and contribute to institutional

C. M. N. Mehrotra (Ed.). *Teaching and Aging.* New Directions
for Teaching and Learning, no. 19. San Francisco: Jossey-Bass, September 1984.

well-being at the same time. While we will make some suggestions specifically applicable to senior faculty, we believe that the most effective, long-range solution to concerns related to this age group is a developmental framework for *all* faculty. Without this framework, some of the problems associated with older faculty will only be larger in number and more serious in the future than they are today. Actually, to ask "What shall we do about older faculty?" is to ask the wrong question. Professionals who are highly developed will likely be effective and productive, no matter what their age. The more insightful question is, "What can be done to help faculty members who are not engaged in movement and growth?"

It is true that there have been some attempts in recent years to put into place personnel policies and faculty development programs that are responsive to the changing professional and personal needs of faculty. What is missing from most of these plans, however, is a thoughtful theoretical framework. This absence of a theoretical base tends to result in piecemeal actions and expedient measures rather than in steps that are truly responsive to the human issues involved.

Further, the absence of a sound theoretical framework in personnel policy leaves the institution open to uninformed criticism. In today's higher education arena, everyone — lay citizen, educator, legislator, student, and parent — is sure he or she has the solution to every educational problem. If there is no explicit theoretical base by which higher education can articulate and defend its policies, it has no footing on which to stand to respond to these critics.

In this chapter, we will (1) provide a brief discussion of theories by Erik Erikson and by Jane Loevinger and suggest ways in which they relate to faculty at different points in their careers; (2) apply the theories to several areas of administrative practice; and (3) identify some of the implications for persons in positions of administrative leadership.

Erikson's psychosocial perspective gives us insight into what issues will be central to the individual at a given time, as well as into what the fundamental focus of his or her decisions will be, while Loevinger's cognitive developmental theory assists us in determining how the person will interpret those issues and what the reasoning process regarding them will be. Through these theoretical lenses, the institution can view its members, know who they are, and understand how they are developing, as well as how policies and procedures can contribute to or retard that developmental process. The theories also give the individual faculty member both a position from which to engage in self-examination regarding his or her own functioning and a perspective from which to analyze the institution.

The Erikson Developmental Theory

Erikson's theory, as charted in Figure 1, describes the stages individuals experience as they move through the life cycle. It gives a greater understanding of professors as they move from the position of neophyte instructors through the process of settling down and becoming a mature part of the institutional establishment. Erikson's notion that "development emerges from the interaction of the person's internal growth with external societal demands" (Widick and others, 1978, p. 2) describes the circumstances in which faculty members continuously attempt to perform their varied roles in teaching, research, and service and at the same time balance institutional demands that sometimes seem incongruent with the developmental process.

Although identity in Erikson's original scheme is something to be dealt with during adolescence, the issues surrounding this phase actually go on throughout an individual's life, particularly when a person faces a major transition (Schlossberg, 1978). It is thus with identity that we begin our description of Erikson's theory and the polar attitudes of the stages of development.

Identity Versus Role Confusion. For most young faculty members, the acceptance of a position in an institution of higher learning marks a major transition, even though the environment is already a familiar one given their lengthy experiences as students. This contrasts sharply with persons who choose nonacademic vocations and move into a new environment such as in industry or business. While the environment of academia may be familiar, the role new faculty members take on is significantly different from what they have experienced before.

Since career choice in our society plays a large part in the determination of who one is, this initial attempt at establishing oneself in the academic community is crucial. The failure to come to grips early on with questions of identity hinders a person in the development of other qualities associated with adulthood and results in role confusion. According to Erikson, development is epigenetic, meaning that each stage builds on the previous ones — the developmental tasks of each stage must be resolved before one can successfully move to the next one. Thus, we can see that if faculty members are not able to resolve issues related to identity, they will be stymied in further growth and development.

Intimacy Versus Isolation. While the implications of this stage seem greater for personal development than for professional growth, there is sufficient application to career development for us to address the issue. Certainly the need to commit oneself "to concrete affiliations and partnerships and to develop the ethical strength to abide by such

Figure 1. Epigenetic Chart

Old Age								Ego integrity vs. despair
Adulthood							Generativity vs. stagnation	
Young Adulthood						Intimacy vs. isolation		
Adolescence					Identity vs. role confusion			
School age				Industry vs. inferiority				
Play age			Initiative vs. guilt					
Early childhood		Autonomy vs. shame, doubt						
Infancy	Basic trust vs. mistrust							

Source: Erikson, 1963.

commitments" (Erikson, 1963, p. 263) is central to one's operating effectively in an institution that values collaboration and cooperation. Individuals who fail to connect and form meaningful relationships with others, whether students or other faculty members, risk separation and avoidance of commitment to partnerships, resulting in a loss of a sense of belonging in the institutional milieu.

Generativity Versus Stagnation. Perhaps the most salient stage for considering the issues related to senior faculty is the stage of generativity and its opposite, stagnation. A description of the generative person might indeed be the description of the ideal faculty member: creative, productive, and concerned for the next generation. Further, Erikson (1963) suggests that adults *need* to teach, and he describes generativity as "encompassing the evolutionary development which has made man the teaching and instituting as well as the learning animal" (p. 266). This "need to be needed" and "concern in establishing and guiding the next generation" serve as powerful motivators for the individual at this stage of development.

Integrity Versus Despair. The last stage becomes more important in higher education as the median age of faculty increases. The professor who reaches the stage of integrity is ready to defend the dignity of his particular life style. He can view his teaching career with equanimity and composure, assured that, on balance, good decisions outweigh bad ones.

Where integrity is not developed, the older faculty member is characterized by a helplessness and hopelessness, and a void of creativity that engender cynicism and noninvolvement with his or her younger associates.

The Loevinger Developmental Theory

Now that we have taken this brief look at Erikson's theory, let us turn to the work of Loevinger on ego development. She presents an integrated model of human development in which the ego is described as the master trait, encompassing "interpersonal relationships, moral and ethical development, and cognitive complexity" (Knefelkamp and others, 1978, p. 69). While Erikson's theory is age-related to a certain extent, Loevinger's model is applicable to all ages, allowing us more flexibility in describing diverse characteristics of faculty without regard to chronological age. As with Erikson, the stages are regarded as sequential, invariant, and hierarchical.

There are seven positions in Loevinger's scheme that relate to adults: self-protection, conformism, self-awareness, conscientiousness, individualism, autonomy, and integration (Loevinger, 1976). A few adults, according to the theory, remain in the self-protective stage, although the majority are at the conformist or conscientious stage or in transition between the two (a level she calls *self-aware*).

While there is very little research on the ego levels of faculty members, a study of a very small sample of faculty and administrators found that their scores were only slightly higher than their students, most of whom were at the conformist or conscientious stage (Weathersby, 1977).

The stages and levels of ego development as identified by Loevinger that are applicable to faculty members are described in the paragraphs that follow.

Self-Protective Stage. The faculty member at the self-protective stage tends to use rules to his or her own advantage and satisfaction. The major concern is not to get caught, and self-criticism is not in his or her range of thinking. This professor looks at things in terms of win or lose—what one person gains, another loses—and tends to be manipulative, opportunistic, and exploitative.

It is likely that there are only a few faculty members at this stage. At the same time, many people, especially those who are only at the next higher stage or two, will frequently act in self-protective ways when they are frightened and under pressure. Faculty members who are at a higher stage, such as the autonomous stage, may still behave in self-protective ways in an environment that does not encourage and foster growth and development. They may protect themselves while not being "self-protective."

Conformist Stage. Loevinger describes the conformist stage as characterized by an insensitivity to individual differences, a reliance on clichés, and a propensity to stereotyping. The individual follows the rules and regulations because the group does and because he or she fears group disapproval. A sense of belonging is extremely important at this stage, and superficial niceness is often found.

Since Weathersby's research (1977) on faculty and Loevinger's findings on adults generally indicate that many professors are probably at this stage, it is important to consider ways in which this level of thinking might manifest itself in the educational environment. Certainly the tendency to stereotype, to measure everyone by one standard, and to desire the approval of one's peers is common in our institutions. Again, the instinct for survival tends to cause a faculty member to give the institution what it demands. Individuals at this level will have an inclination to stick with safe and secure ways of doing things and will resist entrepreneurship and risk taking. Thus, the organization is denied the creativity and inventiveness so important to institutional effectiveness.

Self-Aware Level. As self-awareness increases, faculty members begin to move from the conformist to the conscientious stage. While the self-aware level is a transition in a theoretical sense, "it appears to be a stable position in mature life" (Loevinger, 1976, p. 19). During this transition there is an increased acceptance of multiple perspectives and alternative solutions to problems. The individual is able to allow for exceptions and contingencies, thereby increasing his or her range of responses and behaviors to given situations.

Increasing pluralism in the faculty as well as in the student population places pressure on the faculty member to be able to respond in a variety of ways and to see others' points of view. Self-awareness on the part of faculty members becomes essential if the organization is to be representative of the larger society and capable of contributing to the solution of problems.

Conscientious Stage. Faculty members at the conscientious stage are characterized by a strong sense of responsibility, a concern for communication, and a feeling for others. They are able to look at their own goals and engage in self-evaluation by their own internalized set of standards. Mutuality in interpersonal relations is possible for persons at this stage, allowing for collaborative and cooperative projects. The impact of the person and the institution on society may be grasped by a faculty member who sees what he or she does in the larger social context.

Individualistic Level. Again, the transition from the conscientious stage to the autonomous stage represents a time in which faculty members are acquiring new and qualitatively different ways in which to interact with the environment. At this transitional level, they are more tolerant of themselves and others and come to recognize individual differences and greater complexities of circumstances. There is an increased ability to deal with paradox and contradiction and a building of tolerance for ambiguity.

Faculty members operating at an individualistic level may at times be able to deal with the institution in less stressful ways as they are able to understand the complexities of varying situations. They have more avenues available for making conscious choices as well as a capacity for selecting which issues to deal with.

Autonomous Stage. Persons attaining autonomy are able to cope with the conflicting demands placed upon them by society, community, employer, family, and self. They are able to integrate ideas that appear incompatible and deal with the resulting conflict. Self-fulfillment becomes a personal goal. A high tolerance for ambiguity and conceptual complexity are signs of this stage. Respect for the need for autonomy on the part of others is a hallmark of these persons, and emotional interdependence is acknowledged as inevitable.

It is faculty members at this stage who will be most concerned about and able to build community in the institution: Individuals who can maintain their own sense of self-worth, feel autonomous, and successfully deal with conflict, while at the same time acknowledging and respecting the needs of others, can contribute immeasurably to the success of the educational endeavor.

Integrated Stage. This is the most difficult stage to describe, partly because it is so rare. A new element in the integrated individual is a consolidation of identity that enables the person to transcend conflict and to "live intensely in the present" (Loevinger, 1976, p. 418). In Loevinger's words, the integrated stage represents a longing for and "an opening to new possibilities" (p. 26).

This stage represents the kinds of characteristics a few faculty members may achieve and all of us may aspire to: openness to change, an ability to perceive reality accurately, the capacity for both abstraction and concreteness, a capability of spontaneity, an ability to transcend contradictions and polarities, and an increased objectivity and reflective detachment.

The foregoing description of Erikson's and Loevinger's theories makes no pretense of being an exhaustive treatment. It is, rather, an introduction, focusing on those descriptors that are most applicable to faculty roles. It is important to know that, in actuality, development occurs along a continuum and that the stages are rarely as discrete as they may appear at first glance. Further, the transitions between stages or levels are of tremendous importance. As is true when the caterpillar emerges from the cocoon, the time of transition is one that is filled with potential for growth as well as great vulnerability.

Applications in Administrative Practice

Attempts to make specific application of developmental theory in administration are fraught with danger. The human spirit is not characterized by neat categories, and the unending stream of human subtleties are better captured by the poet than by the researcher. Further, the role of colleges and universities and the nature of the learning process itself do not lend themselves to prescription.

In spite of these reservations, we believe that developmental theory can be used as a source of insight into institutional and faculty effectiveness, so long as theory is used only as a way to illuminate thinking and maintain a sober respect for the uniqueness of each individual. Erikson once said, "We must take our theories with serious playfulness and with playful seriousness" (Fowler, 1981, p. xiii). It is in this spirit that we present some examples of applications that may be a helpful point of departure as administrators reflect upon issues related to faculty.

There are five environmental characteristics that can facilitate development. Growth is fostered "by an environment which allows for (1) experimentation with varied roles; (2) the experiencing of choice; (3) meaningful achievement; (4) freedom from excessive anxiety; and (5) time for reflection and retrospection" (Widick and others, 1978, p. 7).

A helpful overlay to these characteristics is Sanford's (1966) notion of "challenges and support." He suggests that persons have the opportunity to learn and develop when they are presented with challenges that cause some disequilibrium. The learning is more likely to occur when the persons also have adequate support in the environment, so that they do not experience a level of anxiety that might make any movement unlikely.

These five characteristics of a facilitative environment, with the concept of challenges and support, can serve as a useful framework for the administrator as he or she works with faculty in three key areas: faculty planning and evaluation, tenure and promotion, and professional development.

Faculty Planning and Evaluation. Defining those exact responsibilities on which a faculty member is to be evaluated is a planning process that can be used in a developmental way. A helpful practice is for the administrator (a department chair, for example) to conduct planning sessions at the beginning of the year with each member of the faculty. After some discussion as to the needs of the department and the faculty member's individual interests, that same faculty member can develop a planning document detailing his or her goals for the year and the criteria by which he or she can be evaluated. In the same planning session, the chair can attempt to correlate what the faculty member does with the developmental tasks (spoken or unspoken) of his or her stage. For example, it may be better to have a faculty member at the conformist stage teach advanced courses, rather than introductory offerings, since the teaching of higher-level courses is often considered more prestigious. The conformist may be very concerned about what the group thinks; hence, he or she may truly have a need to teach these courses.

In contrast, the faculty member who has achieved generativity may well find it satisfying to teach and mentor beginning students.

This person's identity is not tied up with what colleagues regard as the more prestigious courses to teach.

These other examples may be helpful to the administrator:

- A fifty-eight-year-old sociology professor who appears to be grappling with his own aging process could participate in the establishment of courses for retired persons or conduct research in the area of gerontology
- A nursing instructor of child-bearing age could teach the obstetrics courses in the curriculum
- A faculty member who received her doctorate while she was in her late forties could teach students in the institution's adult degree program

In the examples given here, the negotiating process provides opportunities for faculty members to engage in reflection about their responsibilities. They have some choice about these duties and are challenged to try out new roles that relate to their developmental concerns. Faculty members should not experience excessive anxiety: They have a role in the planning process, and there is clear agreement regarding their responsibilities. Chances of their experiencing success should be increased because the responsibilities relate to their own interests.

In this process, the chair needs to be particularly watchful for cues that indicate the faculty member is in transition from one stage to the next. This is the time of greatest vulnerability for this person, and thus he or she needs strong support. At the same time — and this can be an exciting aspect of the process — the transition may be the time when the person has the greatest energy to accomplish certain goals. For example, a faculty member serving for the first time as head of a key committee in a professional association may need to have more time than usual allotted to this responsibility, since success could be an important ingredient in establishing his or her professional and personal identity.

Knowledge of developmental theory helps the administrator see not only the potential associated with this planning process but the pitfalls as well. The conformist professor, when asked to draft a plan of work for the year, may well include goals and activities not particularly related to the genuine needs of the institution. In such cases, the administrator has to be more directive in guiding the process: He or she pushes for agreement on work that the institution needs the faculty member to do, but does so in a respectful, supportive way.

At the end of the year, when the evaluation process takes place, the faculty member and the chair use the planning document as a guide to review the professor's work and accomplishments for the year. This process should be a blend of caring and straight talk. The chair must bear in mind that faculty members who are having difficulty coping with the issues of the stage they are in, or who are in transition from one stage to the next, are particularly vulnerable and fear criticism and failure.

At the same time, promoting development does not mean all evaluation is positive. To say a person did a good job teaching when that is not true is neither good administrative practice nor growth-producing. On the other hand, when a person has been challenged to stretch a bit by teaching a new course and has done poorly, any criticism should be tempered accordingly. Necessarily negative evaluation provided in a caring, respectful way can be an incentive for genuine growth.

Tenure and Promotion. Effective administrative practices in the tenure and promotion area begin with careful attention to the starting point: the hiring process. The chair should be clear and aboveboard about the outlook for tenure and promotion. If it is good, he or she should say so, but when it is not, the administrator should say that as well. A discussion of present and future enrollment trends, the institution's financial picture, and recent experiences of other faculty in the tenure and promotion process should be part of the procedure. Care should be taken not to tie tenure exclusively to faculty performance, since the denial of tenure is often due solely to institutional constraints. Such a discussion can set a tone of trust and honesty with the faculty member and thereby contribute to a developmental environment.

Once the faculty member is on board, the chair can review the formal criteria for tenure and promotion and can work with the new faculty member in planning the emphasis of the professor's work. During the probationary period, for example, the proportion of time to be allotted to different responsibilities can change. In the first and second year, teaching may be the most important task as the faculty member establishes himself or herself in the department and with students. In the next year the chair may be able to decrease the faculty member's teaching load so that he or she can carry out major research efforts.

How can developmental theory be helpful in the difficult circumstances caused by denial of tenure? In some such instances, the administrator may not do anything differently, but at least the theory helps him or her to understand what is happening in the interaction with faculty, to be more attuned to the dynamics involved, and to provide assistance in more informed ways.

Let us consider the case of an administrator (a dean, for example) who has decided to give notice of nonrenewal to two tenured professors because of program reduction. All of the dean's explanations regarding enrollment shifts and the need for reduction in force probably will be understood very differently by the professor at a self-protective stage from the manner in which the administrator intends the message to be heard. This professor will be unable to see the situation in a non-defensive way. He or she will see the decision as a personal rejection and as a reflection on his or her own competence.

The second professor, one who is at a conscientious stage, has emerged from his or her own embeddedness and is able to view the matter with some detachment. While this professor will not be pleased with the decision, his or her own set of internal rules of evaluation may be such that the professor can say to the dean: "I don't like this decision, obviously. But I suspect if I were in the role of the chief academic officer, I would have done the same thing."

This example points up one of the complicated yet fascinating features of developmental theory. Two people can have the very same experience (in this case, the reception of the message from the dean concerning nonrenewal) yet, because they are are different levels, literally can have different experiences. As Perry (1970) pointed out, we make meaning in ways consistent with our view of ourselves and of the world.

Professional Development. Professional development is not technically an administrative area in the same sense as are the previous two we have discussed. But it merits our attention because professional development can be a potent strategy for achieving the effectiveness of the persons who staff the institution. Further, it is a programmatic response to the developmental issues we have raised and provides "handles" that the administrative leadership can use in creating a generative environment.

Professional development is the process whereby all persons in the institution — faculty, administrators, student services persons, and support staff — are provided opportunities to develop as persons and to enhance their competencies in carrying out their responsibilities. It is far more comprehensive than reliance on such things as sabbaticals and travel to professional meetings. It does, however, *include* these, as well as seminars, workshops, professional reading, formal courses, support groups, and related activities. But professional development in the generative institution is more than that: It is a way of operating. All of the administrative interaction with faculty — in faculty evaluation, in tenure and promotion, in whatever area — should be professionally developmental.

Planning and implementation of professional development must be done collaboratively, rather than imposed by the administrative leadership. True, getting people to participate, particularly, those who need it most, can be a problem. But when a program is designed to connect with people's developmental interests and when it occurs in a generative setting, broad-based participation can become the norm.

There are various approaches administrators can use in helping faculty begin to think about their own development. We have found that an effective and nonthreatening way to do this is to work with faculty in an effort to improve teaching practices. As faculty members come to understand the stages and issues confronting their students, they have an increased awareness of their own development.

The Special Role of Leadership

"'I have to be practical,' presidents have said to me, as if practicality excluded thought, foresight, and vision." This comment was made by George Keller (1983, p. 174) after he interviewed scores of administrators on their use of strategic planning. How practical is our argument that the personnel policies for faculty and the resultant administrative practices should recognize and respond to the changing developmental needs and concerns of the persons who staff the institution?

We believe it is both possible and practical. We agree with the comment made by Peters and Waterman (1982) in their study of excellence in major American corporations: "Much of our discussion has verged on the high-sounding. . . . It is high-sounding, but at the same time it is simply practical" (p. 86). One of the reasons it is practical, in the excellent companies they studied, is that there was a "loose-tight" quality in personnel management. There was a "coexistence of firm central direction and maximum individual autonomy" (p. 318). The companies provided great flexibility and support for the staff, but at the same time there was a strong, even obsessive, insistence on a few core values, quality of effort, and solid results. The suggestions we have made in this chapter assume the same level of accountability and expectations of excellence in colleges and universities that Peters and Waterman describe in private businesses.

What kind of leader can foster values that promote generativity? We believe Burns (Peters and Waterman, 1982) has captured it best in his discussion of "transforming leadership" as "leadership that builds on man's need for meaning, leadership that creates institutional purpose" (p. 82). According to Burns, this kind of leadership, "unlike naked power wielding, is . . . inseparable from followers' needs and goals" (p. 83).

This is not really a surprising conclusion. Colleges and universities have always said that development of the student is their main purpose. We recommend that a similar concern for the developmental needs of faculty be embraced as a central concern of the institution also. What this calls for — to return to Erikson — is generativity on the part of the faculty and administration. We suggest that administrators and faculty who do not behave in generative ways with each other cannot be generative with their students. Such an institutional stance forces those of us in higher education to ask ourselves to be clear about what our purpose is, or to phrase it another way, "What business are you really in?" (Naisbitt, 1982, p. 85). The decline of the railroads in this country has been explained as their failure to realize that they were not in the railroad business but in the transportation business. By the same token, if colleges and universities are in the business of information transmission, then we risk imminent obsolescence; technology and other providers can do it more efficiently than we can. But if we are in the human development business, then we have a chance — and a reason — to survive and prosper.

In the past, human development theory was not at a refined enough level to enable us to make direct applications in administrative practices. This is no longer the case. Developmental theories set forth by persons like Erikson (1963), Loevinger (1976), Kohlberg (1969), Perry (1970), and Fowler (1981) are at a level mature enough to provide clear guidelines for teaching and curriculum development and for administrative practices. "The beginning point is self-consciousness for the organization. It is knowing the place for the first time, understanding what business you are in, or want to be in, and deciding what is central for the health, growth, and quality of the organization" (Keller, 1983, p. 75).

This self-consciousness, this knowing that goes beyond what Polanyi (1966) calls "tacit knowing," is a critical first step if an institution is to become more generative in its dealing with faculty. Naisbitt (1982) reminds us of how potent this self-consciousness about stance is in affecting the day-to-day decisions of an institution. He notes that the criminal justice system has tried to operate, until recent years, under a rubric of rehabilitation. He then goes on to make this critical point:

> During the 1970s, the operating framework slowly changed from rehabilitation to punishment, and that is today's prevailing paradigm. That's why we see — in many or most of our states — mandatory sentencing, the death penalty coming back strongly,

more adolescents treated as adults, more prisons being built, and so forth. Now, throughout our vast law and justice system involving the police, the courts, and the prisons, the millions of decisions and judgments that are made every day are greatly influenced by the operating framework. If that framework is rehabilitation, those millions of decisions tend to be shaped in that direction. If, on the other hand, as is the case today, those judgments are made under a punishment paradigm, they move the law and justice system in an altogether different direction [pp. 94–95].

Thus, the shared perceptions regarding the mission of a college or university have a potent influence in shaping the judgments made as administrators and faculty carry out their work. If the agreed-upon purpose of the institution is generativity and human development, then "all of those collective judgments and actions will be very different indeed" (Naisbitt, 1982, p. 95).

Let us turn to another question. Can an administrator who is at Loevinger's self-protective or conformist stage be effective in contributing to the growth of a faculty member who is at a higher stage? Can an administrator who has not achieved identity, as Erikson has described it, be generative, particularly with a faculty member who is at a higher level than he or she is? In the strictest sense of the theory, the answer is probably no. At the same time, we should bear in mind what Erikson suggests about how to use theory. We should not be hamstrung by the stages he, Loevinger, and others have devised or use them in ways that make our interaction more difficult. The most important contribution developmental theory makes to us is not as a strict map directing specific day-to-day actions, but rather as a means of illuminating our understanding of our sometimes chaotic and stressful lives. For the administrative leader, the theory quickens his or her understanding of how faculty members make meaning of their careers, of administrative actions, and of institutional practices.

The effective administrative leader is one who will be sensitive to the developmental issues being addressed by faculty members, utilize the energy generated through the resolution of those issues, and provide them with the nurturance, support, and encouragement they need in a climate that values the developmental process. Such an institutional stance of generativity can only be created by administrators who are aware of and working on their own personal growth and development.

44

References

Carnegie Council on Policy Studies in Higher Education. *Three Thousand Futures: The Next Twenty Years for Higher Education.* San Francisco: Jossey-Bass, 1980.

Erikson, E. H. *Childhood and Society.* (2nd ed.) New York: Norton, 1963.

Fowler, J. W. *Stages of Faith: The Psychology of Human Development and the Quest for Meaning.* Harper & Row, 1981.

Keller, G. *Academic Strategy: The Management Revolution in American Higher Education.* Baltimore, Md.: Johns Hopkins University Press, 1983.

Knefelkamp, L., Parker, C. A., and Widick, C. "Jane Loevinger's Milestones of Development." In L. Knefelkamp, C. Widick, and C. A. Parker, (Eds.), *Applying New Developmental Findings,* New Directions for Student Services, no. 4. San Francisco: Jossey-Bass, 1978.

Kohlberg, L. "Stage and Sequence: The Cognitive-Developmental Approach to Socialization." In D. A. Goslin (Ed.), *Handbook of Socialization Theory and Research.* Chicago: Rand McNally, 1969.

Loevinger, J. *Ego Development: Conceptions and Theories.* San Francisco: Jossey-Bass, 1976.

Naisbitt, J. *Megatrends: Ten New Directions Transforming Our Lives.* New York: Warner Books, 1982.

Perry, W. G., Jr. *Forms of Intellectual and Ethical Development in the College Years.* New York: Holt, Rinehart and Winston, 1970.

Peters, T. J., and Waterman, R. H., Jr. *In Search of Excellence: Lessons from America's Best-Run Companies.* New York: Harper & Row, 1982.

Polanyi, M. *The Tacit Dimension.* New York: Doubleday, 1966.

Sanford, N. *Self and Society.* New York: Atherton Press, 1966.

Schlossberg, N. K. "Five Propositions About Adult Development." *Journal of College Student Personnel,* Sept. 1978, pp. 418–423.

Shulman, C. H. *Old Expectations, New Realities: The Academic Profession Revisited.* AAHE-ERIC Higher Education Research Report No. 2. Washington, D.C.: American Association for Higher Education, 1979.

Weathersby, R. "A Developmental Perspective on Adults' Uses of Formal Education." Unpublished doctoral dissertation, Harvard University, 1977.

Widick, C., Parker, C. A., and Knefelkamp, L. "Erik Erikson and Psychosocial Development." In L. Knefelkamp, C. Widick, and C. A. Parker (Eds.), *Applying New Developmental Findings.* New Directions for Student Services, no. 4. San Francisco: Jossey-Bass, 1978.

Charles S. Claxton is associate professor in the Department of Curriculum and Instruction and a member of the staff of the Center for the Study of Higher Education at Memphis State University.

Patricia H. Murrell is professor in the Department of Counseling and Personnel Services and a member of the staff of the Center for the Study of Higher Education at Memphis State University.

The stereotypes of agism can cause colleges and universities to minimize the development needs of established faculty members.

The Changing Development Needs of an Aging Professoriate

Roger G. Baldwin

The higher education community, like the nation as a whole, is beginning to show more interest in its older citizens. As the average age of the professoriate increases, colleges and universities have begun to realize that their futures depend not only on how well they prepare the next academic generation but also on how well they maintain the vigor and productivity of current faculty members. Deans, department chairpersons, and faculty development directors are all wondering how best to enhance the work life and career development of college teachers. How can higher education keep aging veteran professors engaged in their work so they will remain effective teachers and positive role models for their students and younger colleagues?

Theoretically, faculty development is intended to enhance the performance of all professors of every rank. It should enable professors to utilize their strengths and overcome their weaknesses. Too often, however, older faculty members are casually written off as "set in their ways," "out of touch," or, worst of all, "deadwood." These agist stereotypes can cause colleges and universities to minimize the development needs of established faculty members and to overlook the special competencies they have to offer. Exactly the contrary should be true: A

C. M. N. Mehrotra (Ed.). *Teaching and Aging*. New Directions
for Teaching and Learning, no. 19. San Francisco: Jossey-Bass, September 1984.

primary objective of faculty development should be to help college professors age successfully.

In recent years, observers of the academic profession have recognized that faculty careers evolve over time as professors mature, gain experience, and revise their interests and professional objectives. Models of the academic career (Hodgkinson, 1974; Baldwin, 1979a; Furniss, 1981) may differ in emphasis or timing, but they generally agree that professors progress through a series of sequential career stages characterized by different demands, motivations, rewards, and professional development needs. Research focusing on academics at different ages and levels of experience (Pelz and Andrews, 1966; Fulton and Trow, 1974; Ladd and Lipset, 1975; Baldwin, 1979b), though limited, tends to concur with the assumption that beginning professors differ from college teachers at mid career and that senior faculty nearing retirement vary in important ways from their younger colleagues.

Unfortunately, policies and programs designed to foster the continuing professional development of faculty members frequently ignore these important distinctions. An assumption somewhat akin to the old adage, "What's good for General Motors is good for the nation," is implicit in many faculty development initiatives. It might read, "What's good for one college professor is good for all college professors." Unfortunately for all concerned, developmental opportunities that offer the same support to all college teachers regardless of their stage in the academic career, their prior experience, or career objectives are likely to be marginally successful at best.

Indeed, the faculty development movement is currently undergoing reexamination. This current assessment has been stimulated by the limited level of participation in formal development opportunities — Geis and Smith's 1979 study found that only 25 percent of faculty made use of formal professional development programs — and by the sense that these programs "often do not satisfy genuine faculty needs" (Brookes and German, 1983, p. 3). Moreover, it seems all the more urgent that efforts toward faculty development must meet the objectives of a diverse range of college professors if they are to justify their existence in today's period of restricted resources.

Up to now, much of the activity under the faculty development rubric has concerned the improvement of instructional techniques, course design, the use of educational technology, new evaluation procedures, and opportunities for acquiring new knowledge in one's field of specialization. These forms of support are especially beneficial for young professors whose skill in the classroom and information base need to be enhanced. Frequently, new professors, fresh from graduate school, learn to perfrom their duties by trial and error. Guidance on successful techniques for lecturing, leading discussion groups, and testing can certainly ease their adjustment to teaching. Discussions on effective time management, together with small-grant support to initiate new scholarly endeavors, can also help novice faculty members make a smooth transition from the role of doctoral student. Occasional programs to orient new academics to their institution — its organizational structure, mores, and the services it offers to faculty — can likewise bring their involvement in the academic enterprise up to full speed more quickly.

A faculty member at a later point in his or her career can benefit from similar opportunities to enhance professional performance. However, faculty development, as it is commonly conceived, overlooks other significant academic career needs that emerge later in the work life a college professor. This chapter examines those needs and their implications for initiatives in faculty development.

Faculty Career Development: Changing Needs

Current thinking about career development emphasizes the desirability of continued professional growth, of new learning, and of change in roles and responsibilities (Shulman, 1983). If we accept this view, we recognize that faculty development for seasoned professors must offer new resonsibilities and challenges as well as opportunities to enhance present skills. It is important to help professors strengthen their disciplinary expertise and improve their functioning in the classroom. But as professors age and acquire experience, they also need to vary their professional routine and new activities that permit continuing growth and prevent academic stagnation.

Two groups of established, veteran professors deserve special attention: mid-career professors and senior faculty members nearing retirement. The first group includes faculty members who have been teaching for ten to twenty years. In most cases they have achieved tenure. They are recognized as competent in their disciplines and in the classroom. In spite of their obvious success, however, they are confronted with a dilemma in their careers. As they anticipate another twenty to thirty years in the academic profession, do they maintain essentially the same career path they have traveled to this point? Or do they branch out in new directions (for example, by experimenting with teaching in an interdisciplinary program or by assuming administrative responsbilities) in search of variety and stimulation in their professional lives?

The second group includes faculty who may be regarded as elder statespersons at a college or university. Most are over the age of fifty. Typically, they have worked at their institution for many years. They have risen through the academic ranks to a senior position in their department. Likewise, in many cases they have also served their institution in other important capacities, such as chair of the budget advisory committee or educational policies committee. In addition, they may have served as an associate or acting dean for some years. At this transition point in their careers, they may find their influence on the wane as many of their colleagues retire, as the age gap between themselves and their students widens, and as younger, more up-to-date colleagues assume the important departmental roles that they previously held. Finally, older professors cannot ignore the inevitability of retirement and life beyond the campus as the date of mandatory separation from the institution draws near. It seems clear from these brief descriptions that the professional development needs of veteran faculty members are sufficiently different from the needs of novice professors to deserve separate consideration.

Development Needs of Mid-Career Faculty. Mid-career professors can benefit from opportunities to redefine and enlarge the scope of their careers. In *The Seasons of a Man's Life,* Levinson and others (1978) describe a midlife transition that typically occurs somewhere around the forty to forty-five age range. During this period (which closely parallels the mid-career stage), adults assess their personal and professional achievements and current life situation. Then they revise their long-term goals and make plans for achieving them.

Mid-career faculty members, in order to remain challenged and engaged in their work, need to assess their careers carefully. They should identify new ways to incorporate variety into their employment routine. Whatever their field of expertise, mid-career faculty members need opportunities to identify new professional endeavors, to experiment with new roles, and generally to expand their overall career horizons. They need to get involved in activities that will keep them excited about their work in higher education.

Development Opportunities for Professors at Mid-Career. Several kinds of professional development opportunities can be particularly valuable to professors at mid career. Because mid career is frequently a turning point or critical period in the academic life cycle, it is often an appropriate time to engage professors in career assessment and planning activities. Many professors, like other midlife adults, wrestle with the familiar question, "Where do I go from here with my life?" But few have a clearly defined, much less satisfying, answer. For some faculty members, a weekend career assessment workshop can provide a vehicle for focusing systematically on the future and making some concrete plans for subsequent advancement. An individualized growth contracting system that encourages faculty members to identify development needs and formulate long-term professional objectives can perform a similar function. Annual or biennial career planning meetings (perhaps under a less presumptuous title) between a professor and his or her department chairperson or dean are another option. They can help mid-career college teachers to focus clearly on the future and make commitments to continued professional growth. This kind of future-directed discussion is too frequently postponed in the press of less important, but urgent, business, such as who will teach Botany 103 next winter term.

Small-grant programs can also enhance the range of growth options open to mid-career faculty. For instance, programs targeted specifically at the forty- to sixty-year-old faculty member (or, alternatively, faculty members with fifteen or more years of service at an institution) can light a spark of enthusiasm in professors who may be turned off by highly competitive funding programs where the payoff rarely equals the required investment of time, energy, and creativity. The small-grant program can stimulate research projects, continued growth in disciplinary fields, solutions to critical institutional problems, and a host of other productive faculty activity. Frequently, the outcomes of a small-grant program far exceed the modest commitment of institutional funds required to support it.

A temporary change of professional scenery is another technique for fostering the career growth of established professors. Movement to a new work environment can bring a faculty member in touch with new colleagues, new resources, and new ideas that can lead him or her into many challenging professional activities. A summer internship in a nonacademic setting (such as a corporation or government agency) can provide an opportunity for a professor to learn new skills and acquire up-to-date knowledge in his or her academic field. It can also acquaint a professor with the kind of work environment his or her students will probably enter after graduation. Less exotic changes of scene may also be professionally invigorating. Faculty exchanges with colleagues from other campuses can offer an enlightening new perspective on teaching strategies, disciplinary issues, and perhaps even institutional policies. A temporary transfer to a different department at one's home institution can likewise facilitate a professor's continued development. The opportunity to teach and take classes in a different (though usually related) academic field can open a person to stimulating new insights, unfamiliar research materials, and, most important, colleagues with whom continued collaboration is relatively easy once one has returned to home base across campus.

Rotating administrative positions or other short-term nonteaching assignments at one's school are other ways to maintain motivation in mid-career faculty members. A term as an assistant dean or grants writer can exercise underutilized faculty talents and give a professor a break from the routine of teaching. Similarly, chairing a task force to improve student retention can provide healthy variety in an academic career. Temporary assignments of this nature can foster a sense of advancement as professors learn new skills they can use in the service of their institution. A broader range of professional skills may also enhance a professor's mobility in the academic job market.

It would be naive to assume that all mid-career faculty members will continue to prosper in the academic profession if they can only receive the proper in-service training or adequate research funding. In some cases, faculty members' career interests move elsewhere while they remain bound physically and economically to higher education. In instances of this sort, development programs will be most beneficial if they can humanely facilitate a "burned out" professor's exit from his or her institution.

Enlightened faculty development can prevent mid-career professors from becoming stuck professionally. Growth opportunities relevant to the developmental needs of veteran college professors can foster positive morale while they motivate faculty members to continue advancing their careers in higher education.

Development Needs of Senior Faculty. Senior faculty members, likewise, have important needs that developmental programs should not ignore. According to Erikson's (1963) landmark theory of human development, as we have seen it described in Chapter Two by Claxton and Murrell, a principal task of adult life is the quest for a sense of generativity — a need to produce something that will outlive oneself, to leave one's mark in some way (Kimmel, 1980). Faculty development programs should facilitate fulfillment of this need by helping senior professors to leave behind a meaningful and lasting legacy.

There are several ways to help faculty members spend their last years on campus purposefully and productively. Professors who have worked at a college for many years typically have a strong sense of loyalty to it and can profit from opportunities to serve their institution in some special capacity. Work with younger colleagues in a supportive, mentor-like relationship can likewise give older professors a sense of achievement through preparation of the next academic generation.

Many older professors find it more and more difficult to relate to students as the age gap between them increases. Hence, some professors need assistance in overcoming this generation gap if their later faculty years are to be rich and rewarding. Finally, senior faculty need support as they prepare for satisfying retirement years. Opportunities to plan for a secure life away from the employing institution can reduce a senior faculty member's anxiety level and maintain morale during his or her remaining years on campus.

Development Opportunities for Senior Professors. Faculty in the "twilight years" of the academic career can benefit from many of the support services helpful to mid-career professors. Senior faculty also deserve special assistance with the professional development needs that are unique to their career stage. Likewise, they have a right to special consideration for the exceptional talents they can offer to their colleges and to their colleagues.

Like their younger counterparts, older professors can profit from opportunities to plan their future career development. Hence, they should be encouraged to participate in career planning workshops, growth contracting systems, or any other efforts to facilitate systematic professional growth. Too often, however, professors nearing retirement are carelessly overlooked for such opportunities. The assumption seems to be that they will not be interested or have too little time left in higher education to justify the investment.

Research (Baldwin, 1979b) does indicate that older faculty members participate in formal professional development programs less often than younger professors do. This finding suggests that a less structured but regular "career planning conversation" with one's department chairperson, for instance, might be a more comfortable and effective career stimulant for a senior faculty member than would a weekend career assessment workshop or an institutionalized growth contracting system. If older professors feel that their department chairperson or dean cares about their development, they are more likely to assume the challenge of professional growth with enthusiasm.

Encouraging senior professors to take on stimulating tasks, especially institutional service, is another way to facilitate their continuing development. A released-time policy that enables faculty members to take on specific assignments beneficial to their college or university can be equally beneficial to the professors involved. It permits them to pursue special interests and exercise particular strengths they have acquired over many years at the institution. For example, a marketing professor could apply her talents to an alumni fund-raising campaign. Similarly, a mathematics professor could become a campus-wide consultant on computer-assisted instruction. As all of these faculty members strengthen their school's educational program, they also increase their own sense of purposeful career advancement.

Opportunities to work closely with colleagues — young and old — comprise another means to keep senior faculty members productively engaged in their work. Novice and veteran professors possess complementary needs. Beginning college teachers must adapt to the intricacies of successful classroom instruction. They also must learn how to balance the demands of teaching, scholarship, and service without being consumed by the process. Established professors with years of experience under their mortarboards are well positioned to help young colleagues ease their way into a successful academic career. Those who have thrived in the academic community can serve as inspiring role models for their less experienced colleagues.

The mentoring process is far from one-sided, however. Policies and projects designed to encourage cooperation among senior and novice faculty can open new growth options for seasoned professors. An older professor can serve informally as a director of new-faculty orientation, master teacher, research design specialist, or career counselor for one or more younger colleagues in a personal, informal capacity. In some institutions, these roles might even be formalized and filled on a rotating basis by highly competent faculty "elder statespersons." Beyond the opportunity to help foundling faculty initiate their careers, these kinds of activities help to prevent older faculty from becoming professionally isolated as many of their cohorts retire. The infectious enthusiasm of new college professors can easily rub off on their senior counterparts, leaving the latter infused with renewed interest and energy for their remaining years in higher education.

Vehicles that bring veteran professors together for dialogue, collegial support, and scholarly collaboration can also renew the careers of senior faculty members. A regular forum such as a biweekly brown bag lunch — sometimes open to the college community, sometimes private — where senior professors share research interests, discuss common readings, or compare teaching strategies is one means to generate exciting interdisciplinary courses and cooperative research initiatives. In addition, a supportive setting of this sort might provide a nonthreatening place for older professors to discuss the growing age gap between themselves and their students. No doubt some useful solutions to the problems of aging faculty would emerge as professors pool their considerable experience. Funding for joint projects involving two or more senior professors can provide career stimulation as well. An especially meaningful activity would be a seminar where older faculty from a range of disciplines share the developments they have observed and the insights they have acquired over long careers in their respective fields. This capstone seminar would help older professors review their careers and bring them to a meaningful conclusion. The main objective of each of these cooperative activities would be to reduce the isolation older professors sometimes experience as well as to open new avenues for continued professional growth.

Faculty vitality late in the academic career no doubt also depends on feelings about the future. Professors are more likely to feel good about their last years of teaching if they can look forward to a secure and interesting retirement. Colleges and universities have a role to play in helping professors prepare for this transition. Retirement planning activities, begun well before the actual separation, can protect fragile faculty morale. Careful financial planning is crucial to successful retirement. Professors can also benefit from assistance with leisure-time planning, information on support services for retired persons, discussions concerning the aging process, and instruction in preventive health care procedures.

Perhaps most important to persons whose identity is closely intertwined with their professional position is the need to know that they will remain valued members of the academic community. Policies granting access to libraries, laboratories, and office space following retirement as well as continued invitations to important academic functions can make the transition from full-time employment much less threatening.

The population of senior faculty members is diverse. McKeachie (1983) concludes from his reading of the research on aging that differences among individuals are likely to increase with age. Hence, no simple prescription can satisfy the professional development needs of older professors. In a nutshell, however, colleges and universities must challenge their veteran faculty to pursue new interests and accept new assignments. If higher education expects little from senior faculty, it will probably get just that. When older professors feel they have a critical role to play in the educational process, they are much more likely to work up to their potential.

Conditions for Encouraging Renewal of Seasoned Professors

When we consider the development needs of mature faculty, it is important to keep in mind a major conclusion McKeachie (1983) draws from the research on aging: Individuals have the ability to change at all ages. A stagnant career often results from a constant, unstimulating environment rather than from the "built-in rigidity" (McKeachie, 1983, p. 9) of older professors.

McKeachie suggests that certain conditions can best enhance the productivity and renewal of seasoned faculty. Among them are freedom, diversity, risk taking, and time pressure. Professors typically enjoy the freedom and personal control over their work lives offered by an academic career. If faculty development is to be effective, professors must be free to choose the growth opportunities that will be most beneficial both to them and to their institution. A variety of activities and responsibilities is essential to keep professors fresh and well-rounded. Risk taking should be encouraged to prevent established college teachers from sinking into a dull routine. Growth requires a willingness on the part of a professor (and his or her institution) to try the uncertain and gamble with failure. In addition, time pressure can act as a source of creative tension that motivates professors to be efficient and productive. Deans and department chairpersons may be reluctant to impose time and productivity demands on established faculty members, but in many cases high expectations from colleagues can provide the incentive that mature professors need in order to continue developing and achieving.

Implications for Faculty Development Policies and Programs

A principal goal of faculty development efforts should be to create the type of work environment that will encourage and reward continuing growth by professors of all ages and levels of experience. In order to serve the needs of established as well as novice faculty, most development initiatives should be sufficiently flexible to respond to the career growth objectives of professors at successive career stages. Usually, general development programs that can be slightly tailored to the interests of veteran professors will prove to be quite useful in encouraging their career growth. In some cases, however, programs aimed specifically at experienced, older faculty members may be a more effective way to meet their professional growth needs.

Conclusion

In a period of fiscal constraint, higher education must use all of its resources, especially its human resources, effectively. It is no longer possible to compensate for the shortcomings of less productive or stale faculty by hiring additional academic staff. Now, more than ever, it is necessary to encourage all professors to continue growing professionally, to remain current in their fields, and to assume different roles and responsibilities as new initiatives are needed to preserve educational quality.

The question is, however, how do we translate our support for faculty development into effective policies and practices that foster professional vitality at all stages of academic life? One important step is to examine our approach to faculty development in light of what we know about adult development and academic careers.

To be effective, faculty development programs must recognize the distinct professional strengths and needs of professors at different points in their careers. These programs must respond to the initial development objectives of beginning professors. But they must also acknowledge that professional development for established faculty should involve more than support for improved teaching and research. The nature of the academic career—repetitive tasks, an abbreviated career ladder (compared to the business world, for example)—requires new challenges and new rewards in order to maintain ongoing faculty vitality (Brookes and German, 1983). Moreover, the evolutionary nature of adult life calls for changed activities and a sense of meaningful progression as aging proceeds.

In sum, the scarce resources that are available to support faculty development will be used most effectively if they are invested in programs that meet specific needs. Colleges and universities will be more vital institutions if they respond to the changing developmental objectives of their professors. Only by helping faculty members to continue growing at each career stage can higher education institutions maintain a vigorous intellectual climate and offer high-quality education.

References

Baldwin, R. G. "Adult and Career Development: What Are the Implications for Faculty?" In R. Edgerton (Ed.), *Current Issues in Higher Education.* Washington, D.C.: American Association for Higher Education, 1979a.

Baldwin, R. G. "The Faculty Career Process—Continuity and Change: A Study of College Professors at Five Stages of the Academic Career." Unpublished doctoral dissertation, University of Michigan, 1979b.

Brookes, M. C. T., and German, K. L. *Meeting the Challenges: Developing Faculty Careers.* AAHE-ERIC Higher Education Research Report No. 3. Washington, D.C.: Association for the Study of Higher Education, 1983.

Erikson, E. H. *Childhood and Society.* (2nd ed.) New York: Norton, 1963.

Fulton, O., and Trow, M. "Research Activity in American Higher Education." *Sociology of Education,* 1974, *47* (1), 29–73.

Furniss, W. T. *Reshaping Faculty Careers.* Washington, D.C.: American Council on Education, 1981.

Geis, G. L., and Smith, R. "Professors' Perceptions of Teaching and Learning: Implications for Faculty Development." Paper presented at the annual meeting of the American Educational Research Association, San Francisco, April 8–12, 1979.

Hodgkinson, H. L. "Adult Development: Implications for Faculty and Administrators." *Educational Record,* 1974, *55* (4), 263–274.

Kimmel, D. C. *Adulthood and Aging.* (2nd ed.) New York: Wiley, 1980.

Ladd, E. C., and Lipset, S. M. *Ladd-Lipset 1975 Survey of the American Professoriate.* Storrs: Social Science Data Center, University of Connecticut, 1975.

Levinson, D. J., and others. *The Seasons of a Man's Life.* New York: Knopf, 1978.

McKeachie, W. J. "Older Faculty Members: Facts and Prescriptions." *AAHE Bulletin,* 1983, *36* (3), 8–10.

Pelz, D. C., and Andrews, F. M. *Scientists in Organizations.* New York: Wiley, 1966.

Shulman, C. H. "Fifteen Years Down, Twenty-Five To Go: A Look at Faculty Careers." AAHE-ERIC Higher Education Research Currents. *AAHE Bulletin,* 1983, *36* (3), 11–14.

Roger G. Baldwin is assistant professor of higher education at the College of William and Mary. His research focuses on the career development of college professors.

Some teaching-related interests and activities may be quite stable over time whereas others may change as a result of developmental processes.

Faculty Age and Teaching

Janet H. Lawrence

A general concern about the aging professoriate and its impact on educational quality pervades higher education. Some researchers believe that developmental processes result in age-related changes in professional interests and activities. Other writers contend that differences between faculty age groups reflect variations in the socialization experiences of demographic cohorts and shifts in the social composition of the faculty. A review of these two interpretations should help educators better understand the effect of faculty age on the teaching-learning environment.

Career Development Models

Several authors (Baldwin and Blackburn, 1981; Hodgkinson, 1974; Sanford, 1971) have created theoretical models of academic career development based largely on the findings from cross-sectional studies. There is little or no empirical evidence that changes in values and performance are age-related and recur across generations of professors. Despite this important limitation (another is the almost exclusive use of male subjects), the career models derived from these studies are useful constructs for synthesizing the research on age-group differences in faculty.

C. M. N. Mehrotra (Ed.). *Teaching and Aging.* New Directions
for Teaching and Learning, no. 19. San Francisco: Jossey-Bass, September 1984.

Career Stages and Dominant Concerns. Most educational researchers agree about the correlation between career stages and the issues that are predominant in the minds and lives of the teachers in those various stages. The newly appointed assistant professor (age twenty-five to thirty) is usually described as someone with an idealized image of himself or herself as a famous scholar and leader in his or her field—that is, Levinson's (1977) "dream." This new professor has definite goals regarding career advancement, and the desire to succeed is a source of career pressure. Professors during this period of their development are often preoccupied with their disciplinary competence and, as a group, they tend to devote a greater portion of time to research; the professional aspects of their life structures are determined largely by the reward context of their institutions (Ericksen and others, 1977).

Next come the "age-thirty transition [and the] time-linked drive toward tenure....[a period in which] the thirty- to thirty-five-year-old faculty member may be torn between five or six equally important and worthwhile tasks, some related to teaching, some to research, and some to his [or her] own family" (Hodgkinson, 1974, pp. 268–269). Sanford (1971) describes this as a period of self-discovery; a time when the individual experiences multiple role demands and must choose from among them. Baldwin and Blackburn (1981) found that professors in this career phase felt they were being pressured to take on new responsibilities, had the lowest scores on career satisfaction, and were more concerned than other groups about personal problems that were interfering with their professional performance.

For those who achieve tenure—we do not know much about those who fail—a period of rebuilding ensues. Associate professors begin to build life structures around new self-images and seek a balance between professional and personal goals (Braskamp and others, 1982). For many, this redefinition involves a change in their identities as disciplinary scholars. Baldwin and Blackburn (1981) report that, as a group, faculty members at this career stage still believe they have contributions to make within their disciplines, but fewer of them regard research as one of their major professional strengths. Sanford (1971) believes that a critical developmental task at this stage is discovery of others— the establishment of genuine relationships with other people. Baldwin and Blackburn's findings suggest the salience of this task as there was a noticeable increase in the proportion of his subjects who, after achieving tenure, thought their rapport with colleagues and students was a professional strength.

A mid-life career transition is experienced by many professors sometime between the ages of thirty-nine and forty-three. Hodgkinson

(1974) believes that at this time many faculty members realize they are not going to become leaders in their disciplines and adjust their career goals downward. Pelz and Andrews' (1976) data may also reflect this trend, as they found productivity had two peaks — one in the late thirties and another in the fifties. Among those who have achieved the rank of professor, there is the realization that the reward structure is primarily economic from achievement of that rank until retirement. This may be the "last chance to get out of teaching" (Hodgkinson, 1974, p. 270). Baldwin and Blackburn's data point out that a high proportion of the "Stage III" professors think their careers are at a standstill and fewer of those at "Stage IV" have aspirations for professional advancement.

Among those professors who successfully resolve the issues of "middlescence," the period of restabilization that follows is marked by a growing identification with their schools; their loyalty stems from a growing love for what it is and "not for what they once dreamed it was or might become" (Hodgkinson, 1974, p. 271). Baldwin and Blackburn's full professors more than five years from retirement (Stage IV) thought their rapport with colleagues was especially strong. Service to their institutions was a major professional strength and a great source of professional satisfaction. Almost all of them (96 percent) said they understood the "mode of operation" at their school.

Hodgkinson (1974) believes that for most people nearing retirement the task is to hang on; Baldwin and Blackburn's subjects within five years of retirement seem to behave in ways that are consistent with this assertion. While these professors were generally satisfied with their careers, they have fewer professional goals, were concerned that their knowledge might be out of date, and showed signs that they were beginning to withdraw from the institution.

Career Stages and Teaching. Researchers have identified career-stage and age-group differences along five dimensions of teaching. First, there appears to be some variance in professors' commitment to the general development of students. Newly appointed and tenured faculty members seem to have more investment in this goal than professors going through the tenure review and those nearing retirement. Faculty from middle age up until a short time before retirement think their rapport with students is one of their professional strengths and they feel comfortable in both their teaching and nonteaching interactions with students (Baldwin and Blackburn, 1981). Persons concerned about the generation gap between older faculty members and traditionally aged undergraduates should find these trends reassuring.

Second, self-assessments of teaching competence are higher among senior professors, and student ratings suggest no age-related decline in performance. More assistant professors (68 percent) in Baldwin and Blackburn's sample reported a "teaching deficiency as one of their major professional weaknesses" and said they discussed teaching concerns with their colleagues. Both of these items showed drops across career stages, beginning with associate professors (Stage III) and continuing until retirement. McKeachie (1983) states that the limited data that are available indicate "student ratings are lower for teachers in their first year or two of teaching but relatively unrelated to age after that" (p. 60).

Third, the beginning academicians report that a high proportion of their time is devoted to teaching and interacting with students; this trend drops among those going through the tenure review but picks up again later (Baldwin and Blackburn, 1981). Ericksen and others (1977) found a similar tendency among subjects in their study of academic careers. Junior professors explained that the weight given to scholarly productivity in promotion decisions was much greater than that given to teaching, and, as a result, a greater proportion of their time was devoted to research. However, Thompson (1971) found an overall inverse relationship between academic rank and time devoted to course preparation and work with students.

Finally, data show differences between career stages with respect to identity as teachers (Fulton and Trow, 1974) and satisfaction derived from teaching (Baldwin and Blackburn, 1981; Ericksen and others, 1977). The apparent discrepancy between these findings could be explained in part by the fact that respondents in the Ericksen study made a distinction between the immediate gratification they experienced in teaching and the more enduring satisfaction they derived from their research. It could also be a matter of timing: Professors may be simultaneously revising their self-images and realizing they have reached the top of the academic ladder.

In addition to these generalizations (which are supported by empirical data), there are important inferences that can be drawn from the career development literature. One might expect some differences across academic ranks and age groups with regard to instructional priorities. Faculty members in the initial stages of their careers might favor early specialization within the discipline and prefer to teach upper-level courses that focus on their narrow areas of interest. Senior professors, as a result of interaction within and improved rapport with a growing circle of colleagues, may perceive a need for a broad knowledge base and press for delay in undergraduate specialization. They may prefer to teach more general and interdisciplinary courses. Subjects in the study by Ericksen and others (1977), for example, said that after the tenure decision they were freer to pursue their individual interests, which were often less central to their discipline and more interdisciplinary in nature.

Untenured professors could experience dissonance with respect to curricular experimentation. On the one hand, they are concerned about the long-term development of students; on the other hand, they need to devote time to those activities that are given priority in tenure decisions. Should they adopt the most parsimonious approach and teach the well-established ongoing courses, postponing until after tenure any major commitment to new course development or revision? Among those who have just received tenure and are feeling the pressure of multiple role demands, there may be resistance to course schedules that meet the needs of new students but erode their control of time.

Demographic Model

A second group of researchers recognizes the existence of age-group differences, but they believe that the variations can be explained largely by cohort flow and general changes in the social composition of a faculty.

A key assumption for these researchers is that people are more malleable during certain periods of their lives; experiences at these times, it is felt, "exert a lasting influence on both beliefs and actions" (Pfeffer, 1983, p. 49). Organizational demographers argue that faculty members who complete their graduate studies and strive to achieve tenure during the same time interval are enculturated with similar values; this group is called a *demographic cohort.* The members' beliefs remain quite stable throughout professors' careers and, as cohorts enter and exit the age strata, the characteristics of each stratum may be altered. Hence, what appear to be age-related changes in values and behavior may actually be the result of cohort flow.

The work of several researchers suggests that early socialization experiences have an impact on academic career patterns (Clark and Corcoran, 1983; Parsons and Platt, 1973; Trow, 1977). Clark and Corcoran, for example, found that professors who were active scholars were more often involved in research as graduate students and were more likely to maintain professionally helpful contacts with peers that would lead to publishing and research opportunities after graduation. Furthermore, the highly productive faculty members maintained high levels of commitment to their roles as scholars.

The importance of graduate experiences and institutional expectations for untenured professors was underscored by an exploratory study of faculty careers conducted at the University of Michigan (Lawrence and Blackburn, 1984). The researchers examined differences in scholarly productivity among three appointment cohorts (1960, 1965, 1970) and three age groups (those born in the 1920s, 1930s, and 1940s). The results showed no correlation between age and number of publications during each of three career periods — preappointment, pretenure and posttenure. However, the data revealed that respondents who were appointed as assistant professors in 1970 were more involved in research as graduate students and during the pretenure period. (At the time of the study, data were not available for more than two years posttenure for this cohort. A follow-up survey is underway that will indicate if this trend is maintained.)

The study findings with respect to promotion experiences suggest that the criteria applied in the tenure decision influenced both the professors' behavior and values. For all the cohorts, there was a significant correlation between respondents' grasp of the criteria and their distribution of effort as assistant professors. The 1970 cohort reported that significantly greater emphasis was given to their research when they were promoted to associate professor. Even under ideal conditions, the weight assigned to scholarship by the 1970 respondents was greater than that found within the 1960 and 1965 cohorts.

A small but critical set of studies has investigated the impact of changes in the sociodemographic composition of a faculty on professors' role patterns, career satisfaction, and affinity for a particular institution. Pfeffer and Moore (1980) demonstrated how staff turnover and tenure levels affect the number and type of role opportunities within a department. McCain and others (1982) and Pfeffer (1983) have examined discontinuities in staff replacement and suggest that generation gaps can lead to conflicts regarding policy and, ultimately, to lack of career satisfaction.

In the study by McCain and others, the researchers found that, as the average age and length of service of a department increased, so, too, did the amount of agreement about what was central to the discipline. The Lawrence and Blackburn (1984) data indicated that the cohort with the most years of service in the university perceived greater departmental consensus regarding tenure criteria. The general conclusion in both studies was that shared values evolve primarily because the professors have had more opportunities to develop a similar outlook and because often those who hold different views leave the institution. Lawrence and Blackburn speculate that the organizational conditions that lead to increased consensus may also create within a faculty subgroup an enhanced identity with a particular institution. They suggest that professors who are from the same demographic cohorts as are administrators may experience the strongest affinity because they hold similar values and are part of the same communication network.

The representativeness and durability of the behavior and values discussed in this section are open to question. The research has been carried out primarily in graduate universities and within a brief time period. Nonetheless, it is important to consider the findings vis-à-vis teaching and the aging professoriate.

Organizational demographers probably would predict that during the next twenty years, age-group comparisons will show professors in their middle years identifying more closely with their roles as scholars. The rationale for the prediction is that, as a result of cohort flow (that is, the 1970 cohort moving into its fourth and fifth decades), the values that characterize these age strata will change. Pfeffer (1983) projects that the 1950 cohort members will continue to identify themselves as teachers up until the time they retire. If the recruitment and tenure criteria continue to stress research, it may well be that the younger and middle cohorts will share similar views about what are key departmental activities, and career satisfaction will be high as a result. Scholarly activities will probably be assigned a high priority, but it does not necessarily follow that commitment to teaching will decline. The research done by Clark and Corcoran (1983) and Fulton and Trow (1974) showed that professors who were productive scholars tended also to be highly involved in their roles as teachers.

Conclusions

The career development literature suggests that, throughout their careers, professors evaluate and redefine their life structures. As a result of these self-assessments, there are differences between age groups in terms of the members' teaching interests, performance, and overall personal investment in their colleges.

Organizational demographers believe that the data accurately reflect faculty preferences for teaching-learning activities that currently exist in most postsecondary institutions. They would, however, urge educators to exercise caution and to review the social composition of a faculty before making generalizations about the age-relatedness of these interests and behavior.

Institutional researchers would be well advised to begin collecting longitudinal data that will help colleges sort out developmental changes from demographic effects. Such information would be helpful to individual professors who wish to better understand themselves, to

64

department chairpersons who advise faculty members, and to administrators who are planning instructional support services or who are revising present practice and policies so as to enhance performance and build upon their existing faculty resources.

References

Baldwin, R. G., and Blackburn, R. T. "The Academic Career as a Developmental Process." *Journal of Higher Education,* 1981, *15,* 598–614.

Braskamp, L. A., Fowler, D. L., and Ory, J. C. "Faculty Development and Achievement: A Faculty's View." Paper presented at the annual meeting of the American Educational Research Association, New York, April 1982.

Clark, S. M., and Corcoran, M. "Professional Socialization and Faculty Career Vitality." Paper presented at the annual meeting of the American Educational Research Association, New York, April 1983.

Ericksen, S., Moore, W., and Lawrence, J. "Merit Dimensions and Teaching in a Graduate University—Faculty Perceptions." Paper presented at the annual meeting of the American Educational Research Association, New York, March 1977.

Fulton, O., and Trow, M. "Research Activity in American Higher Education." *Sociology of Education,* 1974, *47,* 29–73.

Hodgkinson, H. L. "Adult Development: Implications for Faculty and Administrators." *Educational Record,* 1974, *55* (4), 263–274.

Lawrence, J., and Blackburn, R. "Faculty Careers: Maturation, Demographic, and Historical Effects." Paper presented at the annual meeting of the American Educational Research Association, New Orleans, April 1984.

Levinson, D. "The Midlife Transition: A Period in Adult Psychosocial Development." *Psychiatry,* 1977, *40,* 99–112.

McCain, B. E., O'Reilly, C., and Pfeffer, J. "The Effects of Departmental Demography on Turnover: The Case of a University." Unpublished manuscript, University of Iowa, 1982.

McKeachie, W. J. "Faculty as a Renewable Resource." In R. T. Blackburn and R. Baldwin (Eds.), *College Faculty: Versatile Resources in a Period of Constraint.* New Directions for Institutional Research, no. 39. San Francisco: Jossey-Bass, 1983.

Parsons, T., and Platt, G. M. *The American University.* Cambridge, Mass.: Harvard University Press, 1973.

Pelz, D. C., and Andrews, F. M. *Scientists in Organizations.* (rev. ed.) New York: Wiley, 1976.

Pfeffer, J. "Organizational Demography." In L. L. Cummings and B. M. Staw (Eds.), *Research in Organizational Behavior.* Vol. 5. Greenwich, Conn.: JAI Press, 1983.

Pfeffer, J., and Moore, W. L. "Average Tenure of Academic Department Heads: The Effects of Paradigm, Size, and Departmental Demography." *Administrative Science Quarterly,* 1980, *25,* 387–406.

Sanford, N. "Academic Culture and the Teacher's Development." *Soundings,* 1971, *54* (4).

Thompson, R. K. "How Does the Faculty Spend Its Time?" Unpublished paper, University of Washington, 1971.

Trow, M. "Departments as Contexts for Teaching and Learning." In D. E. McHenry and Associates (Eds.), *Academic Departments: Problems, Variations, and Alternatives.* San Francisco: Jossey-Bass, 1977.

Janet H. Lawrence is associate professor of higher education and associate director of the Center for Research on Learning and Teaching at the University of Michigan. Her research focuses on the career development of college professors.

*Retiring professors recognize the university's right and need
to move older faculty out and young faculty in; however, they
feel that they have a right to expect this will be done in a
humane way.*

Personal Perspectives of Academic Professionals Approaching Retirement

*Betty Jane Myers
Richard E. Pearson*

Retirement, while having its unique features, shows general overlap
with other life transitions in terms of the impact it has upon persons.
Nancy Schlossberg (1981) has proposed a model that specifies three factors that play an important role in determining the degree of success
with which individuals resolve the issues raised by life transitions.
These factors are: (1) the characteristics of the transition itself (such as
how much difference there is between pre- and postretirement environ-
ments); (2) the characteristics of the setting within which the transition
occurs (such as how supportive the physical and social contexts are);
and (3) the individual (for example, what the individual's prior expo-
sure to the same or similar transitions is, and the individual's general
level of psychosocial competence).

Against the backdrop of Schlossberg's work and, more specifically, of the findings of many studies that have examined preretirement
issues among workers in many fields (such studies as those by Kimmel
and others, 1978, and by Thurnher, 1974), this chapter presents the

C. M. N. Mehrotra (Ed.). *Teaching and Aging.* New Directions
for Teaching and Learning, no. 19. San Francisco: Jossey-Bass, September 1984.

views of a group of university faculty, all within five years of possible retirement. This discussion makes no pretense of being representative; the persons interviewed were twelve married academics who were affiliated with a large, nonsectarian, private university in the northeast United States. The research methodology was qualitative in nature, centering upon the analysis of semistructured interview data in order to discover common themes and issues voiced by the faculty.

In spite of these limitations, and perhaps specifically because of the study's individual-centered methodology, the perspectives that follow will be useful to those attempting to appreciate the subjective experience of academics and their spouses as they near retirement. Using Schlossberg's work as a broad framework, the discussion centers upon their views of the transition itself, the settings within which the transition was unfolding, and their views of their own characteristics, experiences, needs, and resources.

Views of the Retirement Transition

As the faculty members who were interviewed approached the age of sixty-five, they recognized the need to take stock of themselves and their situation. Asked what retirement would mean to them, most made a distinction between the formal act of retirement and the continuation or discontinuation of their scholarship. A typical comment was: "Even if I leave the university in a few years, I'll never retire. I'll always do research."

Not so hopeful, however, was a woman (now primarily involved in administration) who could not foresee a postretirement activity in which she could be pressed so continually to grow personally and professionally, or in which she would be gratified so completely in meeting responsibilities as she was currently. Despite strong family ties and involvement in leisure activities, she doubted that a challenge as exciting as her work would be found when she carried through on her plan to retire at age seventy.

Coupled with the general desire to continue work on at least a modified basis was another factor that helped to draw the sting of academic retirement: the flexibility currently allowed in timing the event. More than 80 percent of those interviewed intended to remain in their positions until age seventy (assuming that their health would permit), preferring work to other alternatives. This ability to determine when and how they would retire gave them control over an important life event and, it seems, allowed them to postpone a harsh confrontation with an abrupt change in their lives.

Those faculty who thought they would probably leave the university at age sixty-five spoke of both positive reasons (such as improved pension benefits and optimal Social Security payments) and negative ones (such as physical problems or dissatisfactions with the work situation) for choosing the earlier retirement time.

Perceived Losses. Among the negative effects of retirement, participants mentioned regret for the loss of professional stimuli and personal rewards inherent in their current work setting—such stimuli as the interchange of information and ideas; the needs, expectations, and support of colleagues; and the interaction with students; and such rewards as the availability of office space, equipment, and support staff. Being productive would be difficult, they acknowledged, without the personal and material supports that were now a part of their lives.

Such nonwork concerns as the possible loss of physical stamina, decreasing sensory acuity, the illness or death of spouse and friends, and the loss of valued associates because of relocation were neither ignored nor stressed. The participants recognized the likelihood of losses and they acted, or contemplated acting, to eliminate, minimize, or postpone such losses. Preparing in whatever fashion they could, most of those interviewed speculated little about what might happen.

There were, however, areas of real anxiety that revealed themselves during the discussion. The shift from earner to pensioner caused varying degrees of concern to those interviewed because of the influence of inflation. Most uneasy were those who had, or would soon have, college-age children. They felt the constraints of a tight budget even now, and they feared that financial restrictions would limit their retirement satisfaction.

Perceived Gains. While recognizing some changes as having negative implications, the participants anticipated with pleasure the opportunity to emphasize preferred pursuits more than was currently possible. Less demanding schedules would permit an emphasis upon writing, research, or consulting. Many spoke with relish of learning projects, exploration and expression in the arts, increasing physical activities, being close to nature, personal time with family and valued others, and participating in community affairs—certainly no retirement from life.

The majority of those interviewed felt fairly secure financially. In addition to pension and Social Security income, the assets of many included investments, real property, and a working spouse. Much of their assurance derived from their systems of values: They thought they would be able to manage with modest incomes. The following statement is representative: "We don't need a lot of money. We've done the big traveling we wanted to do. Our house suits us and it's ours. We just need enough to feed us, clothe us reasonably, and keep a roof over our heads. We'd want to entertain family now and then and make occasional visits to them. Otherwise, our needs are very modest."

The Role of Values in Retirement Planning

Many of the faculty reported a growing awareness of what was uniquely important as they approached retirement, and this led them to focus their energies and time in order to experience valued activities and relationships.

Transcending all areas of life was the participants' push for mental stimulation and effort. In planning for many aspects of retirement (such as work, leisure, housing, and social interaction), they stressed the importance of maintaining a curious, active mind; one individual spoke for many when he said: "To learn, to be mentally active — this is an asset in retirement. I put together many courses in the field of community education; they could be made into books. My challenge is all the journals and books I'd like to be reading: I just can't keep up."

Closely associated with mental stimulation and effort was a concern for esthetic values. Most of the faculty anticipated supplementing their already considerable knowledge about, and appreciation for, art, literature, crafts, and household arts with active expression in those areas.

Esthetic interest was often linked to social activities, as in attending and discussing plays, operas, and concerns with friends. Cultural interests were also often tied up with feelings of community responsibility. Those interviewed anticipated such activities as planning art shows for civic and religious groups, serving on the boards of cultural groups, and supporting musical and dramatic organizations financially.

In terms of the hierarchies of important associations, the participants typically accorded the first rank to spouse and family. The mate's contributions were noted and appreciated. "She brought interesting people into our lives." "One helps when the other needs it — we've sort of alternated, and we get more done and take on more that way. Each one pushes the other a bit." "He taught our daughters they could do anything they set their hearts on doing."

Although the nuclear family was usually dispersed, participants valued the idea of family. It was clearly an area for altruism and mutuality, and the ground for growing, accepting, and being accepted. "The kids got together by phone (one in New York City, the other in Alaska) to write a song for my sixtieth birthday. When they finally got it together, they called and sang it over the phone in a conference call. I'd say we're closer with them now that they're at arm's length than when they were younger."

For both men and women, a second highly prized context was the world of nature. Expectations focused upon many aspects of natural phenomena and could be catalogued as esthetic appreciation, mental stimulation, physical activity, and spiritual inspiration. "We've always been gardeners, but now it's more than that. It's birds, and scenery, and walking. I really think we may be becoming less interested in people and more interested in nature. Maybe this is a natural way of getting accustomed to withdrawing from the daily interaction with a hell of a lot of... you get a bit battle-fatigued."

A third context, the broader community, figured prominently in the current and anticipated lives of the faculty. The cultural resources of their community were often cited as a major reason for those who had decided to remain in their present location after retirement. Contributing their professional skills and experience to the community (a contribution already being made by over two-thirds of the group) was another civic link. Others contemplated such service after they retired. Also important were the personal contacts possible in religious and service organizations.

Those interviewed liked their metropolitan area for its size (250,000), location, health delivery systems, stores, sporting activities, and housing options. For most, a strong individual-community tie had formed over time. The area had become part of their history, and many were reluctant to leave behind familiar people, institutions, and terrain for distant, unknown locales.

One quarter of the group, however, planned to investigate living in areas where the climate was warmer, where they could live in a community of persons like themselves, or where they could accomplish special projects. It seems these couples felt added impetus to move because, in all but one case, they believed their present home would not be suitable for retirement living. Also, they had lived in several parts of the United States and various countries abroad and believed they would feel readily at home in a new place.

A fourth valued context, the university, emerged as a very important factor in the considerations of the faculty. All the values of personal style, relationships, and activities seemed to unite in the life of the university. For many of those interviewed, there was the expectation that the comings and goings at the university would be of interest and concern to them. The privileges available to emeriti professors (such privileges as library use, study carrels, recreational facilities, reduced prices for university events, inclusion in ceremonies and festive events, recitals, art shows) were recognized and appreciated by those planning to stay in the university area.

They recognized the university's right and need to move older faculty out and young faculty in. They recognized the necessity of moving through this life transition and, in one way or another, echoed the words of one respondent who said, "As children leave the family home, the time will come to move on." However, they believed they had the right to expect that the process would be handled humanely by the university.

Preretirement Programs

The challenge of a preretirement program is to enlist participants in a process of discovering and considering individual alternatives. The content of these programs should proceed from the needs, interests, and personal qualities of the faculty and their important others.

Common Themes and Patterns. When asked what they considered to be the factors that would be important to their future, the respondents talked about specific, expected topics (such as money, health, and housing). However, as their discussions continued, a less obvious agenda, comprised of the following themes, emerged:

- Managing self and adapting to circumstances effectively
- Being in close relationship with spouse, family, and a few close friends
- Surviving professionally (through formal and informal alternatives)
- Making a contribution to others and being needed by others
- Exploring and developing capabilities and relationships.

From these discussions, it was clear that the faculty preferred to be active in determining the important elements of their lives. They desired information regarding alternatives for choice and action. They also looked to the university for signs that they would be both esteemed and cared about and that the mutually gratifying relationship they believed currently existed would continue.

Content and Structure of Programs. What suggestions for the content and structure of faculty preretirement programs can be drawn from the views of this group? Again, the Schlossberg (1981) model provides an organizing framework.

In terms of the transition itself, programs need to focus upon the information (and misinformation) that faculty have about the realities of retirement. Clear, accurate information about the implications of retirement for finances, housing, and health care is vital. Some faculty demonstrated a high level of current, detailed knowledge about these issues. Others seemed to have devoted little energy to examining the implications of retirement for their life situations. It is interesting to note that seminars on investment planning for faculty in their thirties and forties are actually offered by the university, but participation has been minimal. Whether faculty are too busy or too reluctant to think about their later years, one can only speculate.

Beyond implementing activities geared for the faculty as a whole, university policy makers should give consideration to establishing policies flexible enough to allow variation from one person to another in the speed with which retirement occurs and in the degree of change that it actually represents. Some faculty expect to close their office doors and never come back. Others want to hold on to some participation in the academic and social life of the university. Flexible policies and the availability of formal and informal vehicles for involvement in the life of the institution would allow faculty to have some control over the degree of change that retirement imposes upon them.

Since faculty recognize the importance of the university, the family, and the community as settings for their retirement, preretirement programs would do well to focus upon both informational and attitudinal issues with regard to these settings. For example, knowledge of university policies and programs, community health care resources, or transportation alternatives can be useful to those who will stay in their present community. The importance of positive attitudes toward environmental and social support can be highlighted by opportunities to interact with already retired faculty.

Finally, the program should help the preretirees examine the degree to which their personal characteristics and experience can be used in coping with the upcoming transition. What other transitions have they made that share features with retirement? What skills and attitudes have been useful in the successful resolution of past transitions? What are their attitudes toward dependence and independence, and how do those attitudes relate to situations they may confront in retirement? What are the elements of their current identities upon which self-esteem rests? How is retirement apt to affect that identity, and, if the arena within which their self-esteem is maintained is apt to be eliminated or reduced, how can remaining areas be expanded or new outlets developed?

These are important questions for preretirees to confront. Many have done so on their own. For those who have not, a preretirement program that incorporates presentation of information, first-person accounts of already retired colleagues, and small group discussions can at least sensitize faculty to the importance of self-examination and review.

Conclusion

Though the faculty interviewed acknowledged concerns and the possibility of future problems, in general they had a positive, optimistic outlook about retirement. Perhaps the tone of that easy enthusiasm was best expressed by one professor when, with a chuckle, he said, "I hope to be healthy, wealthy, and wise — in that order!"

References

Kimmel, D. D., Price, K. F., and Walker, J. W. "Retirement Choice and Retirement Satisfaction." *Journal of Gerontology*, 1978, *33*, 575–585.
Schlossberg, N. K. "A Model for Analyzing Human Adaptation to Transition." *The Counseling Psychologist*, 1981, *9* (2), 2–18.
Thurnher, M. "Goals, Values, and Life Evaluations at the Preretirement Stage." *Journal of Gerontology*, 1974, *29*, 85–96.

Betty Jane Myers is a doctoral candidate in counselor education at Syracuse University.

Richard E. Pearson is associate professor of counselor education at Syracuse University. His research interests focus upon the nature of social support and the structure of natural support systems.

*With anticipated individual retirement lasting fifteen to
thirty years, effectively utilizing the accumulated experience
of high-achieving professionals presents a national challenge.*

The Academy of Senior
Professionals at Eckerd College

Leo L. Nussbaum

Eckerd College, located on 267 acres of tropical waterfront property in
St. Petersburg on an estuary of the Gulf of Mexico, was founded in
1958 (as Florida Presbyterian) as a free-standing college of the liberal
arts and sciences. One of the declared objectives of the college is to aid
the personal development of humane and competent persons of all ages
so that they may learn, lead, and serve in the local, national, and international realms of a pluralistic and increasingly complex society.

From its inception, Eckerd College has been committed to dis-
tinctiveness. One of its several purposes is to serve persons of all ages,
which in the founding year was not as common a goal among colleges
and universities as it is today. The college also is committed to academic
innovation as one of its distinctive characteristics. This spirit of innovation continues to pervade the institution, from the trustees (as the
governing body) through the faculty and administration to the students.

The Basic Plan

During the early seventies, on the initiative of the administration
and faculty, Eckerd College began to consider a range of programs for
the retired. In 1973, after extended consultation with Sidney Tickton of

C. M. N. Mehrotra (Ed.). *Teaching and Aging.* New Directions
for Teaching and Learning, no. 19. San Francisco: Jossey-Bass, September 1984.

75

the Academy for Educational Development, the trustees established an Academy *for* Senior Professionals–Eckerd College (ASPEC), based on the conviction that experience and mature talents are commodities too precious to waste. The academy provided retired and semiretired individuals an opportunity to meet with peers, and occasionally with faculty and students, to discuss and study topics of mutual interest. ASPEC members conducted seminars on a noncredit basis. Planned to be financially self-supporting from membership fees, the group was, unfortunately, never large enough to make the venture economically viable, and the program was discontinued in 1979.

However, administrators and faculty of the college were persuaded that the basic idea had too much merit to be discarded, so they set about to redefine the academy in the hope of a new beginning. Eckerd's new president, Peter H. Armacost, provided strong leadership and fresh momentum.

After careful planning between 1979 and 1982, administrators and faculty formulated a profile of the Academy *of* Senior Professionals at Eckerd College. While the new name was different only in the preposition, it denoted a basic difference. This time the academy was formed not by the faculty but by senior professionals *for* senior professionals.

The Academy was defined as "an association of those from various professional backgrounds who, having come to the stage of life when they no longer must meet the pressures of regular employment, would like to join with others in comparable circumstances in the realization of personal and shared goals entailing various forms of intellectual, cultural, and service activities" (Committee on Organization, 1980, p. 3).

The Academy of Senior Professionals is devoted to a threefold task: creating an environment of exploration and accomplishment that will attract members with a history of distinguished achievement; providing a climate of continuing intellectual and cultural stimulation; and enabling members to work singly and in groups on projects of personal and social significance.

Central to this plan is a combination of activities that engage members, both in small groups and the Academy as a whole, balanced by activities that meet the distinctive needs of individuals.

The Academy of Senior Professionals at Eckerd College is open to men and women of all races, religions, and nationalities.

The Development Phase: 1980–1982

In the summer of 1980, a full-time director, Lloyd J. Averill, was appointed. His task was to formulate statements of purpose, select a broad-based organizing committee, and prepare an organizational plan more diverse than the original one. Averill spent months conferring with faculty and administrative colleagues at Eckerd College and consulting on a national scale, and then began to formulate certain ideas in a series of drafts, proposals, and plans. The following paragraphs from a widely distributed brochure (Academy of Senior Professionals at Eckerd College, 1980) are representative of the direction these directives took:

> One of the brightest spots in public awareness and social policy is the attention which is being given, by public and private organizations and agencies alike, to older Americans as a broad and enlarging segment of our society, and most particularly to the needs of the older poor among them.
>
> However, very little specific attention is being given to another group of older Americans with distinctive needs of their own: retired men and women who have had distinguished careers in a variety of professional fields, whose need is to have their continuing talent, experience, wisdom, and leadership acknowledged, stimulated, and extended and thus conserved and utilized as a major national resource [p. 3].

In the same brochure, the director announced plans for the Academy: "In response to that need, Eckerd College is preparing to establish, on or about July 1, 1981, an Academy of Senior Professionals whose purposes will be:

- To provide for the association of such persons
- To make resident facilities available to them on the Eckerd campus
- To contribute to their continuing educational interests and growth through a formal curricular program designed by and for them
- To generate the kind of intellectual and professional (especially interprofessional) stimulation which can encourage and extend their continued productiveness
- To provide them with opportunities to continue to be "competent givers" by direct services to each other, to students of traditional college age, to Eckerd faculty, and to important segments in the college's wider public constituencies
- To provide them with the public recognition such activities deserve" [p. 2].

Originally, it was assumed that members would come primarily from the St. Petersburg area and from those professions and careers into which Eckerd College graduates most commonly go: human services (ministry, social welfare), health sciences, law, education, business, government service at all levels, the media, and the arts. Membership was to be open to persons age fifty-five or over who were no longer engaged in full-time professional practice. Candidates were expected to be recognized by peers as distinguished practitioners — imaginative, creative, and inventive in professional practice. They would give evidence of their humane character and moral integrity, and they would pursue their own liberal learning.

During the summer of 1981, Lloyd J. Averill resigned for personal reasons; George M. Schurr was appointed as his successor. Planning and preparation were continued; however, the scheduled opening date was postponed.

A nine-person committee on organization was formed, chaired by Francis H. Palmer, former provost, professor of psychology, and president of Merrill-Palmer Institute. The committee was designed to provide broad representation among persons retired from professions and careers. Members included a university dean of overseas programs who was also a major foundation adviser; an architectural designer and artist; an author and foreign correspondent; a professor of physics; an international rug connoisseur and merchant; a faculty woman from a school of dentistry; a minister, professor, and editor; and a chairman and president of a national corporation.

For many months the committee on organization and its subcommittees met to clarify policy statements, revise drafts on procedures, articulate membership requirements, and prepare a prospectus. The director and the committee then developed a program for the academic year 1982–1983.

The First Year of Program Operation: 1982–1983

The Academy of Senior Professionals at Eckerd College was formally inaugurated on October 31, 1982, with a series of programs for eight consecutive days, involving a list of distinguished speakers. The occasion was also the introduction of a series of programs and events by the Fellows of the academy, who represented a variety of disciplines, such as history, religion, marine science, medical sciences, mathematics, gerontology, and English. The Fellows program continued for several months. It was also the occasion of the first meeting of the eleven-member national advisory board, composed of leaders from education, business, government, health sciences, medicine, demography, arts and sciences, and theology. Their consultation helped to ensure a national perspective as they evaluated plans for the academy and made recommendations regarding structure, organization, and governance. Their assembly also gave the academy the broad media coverage it needed.

The academy opened with a membership of fourteen, seven of whom were members of the committee on organization; charter members were added through June 30, 1983, at which time there were thirty-one. Among the members today are college professors and presidents, physicians, dentists, artists, ministers, business executives, authors, nuclear chemists, engineers, architects, foreign correspondents, and military officers. It was planned that there would be eighty members in the academy as of June 30, 1984.

A monthly publication, *ASPEC Update USA,* was begun; it is now being mailed nationally to more than 2,000 persons and additions to the list are made weekly. Inquiries are received daily by mail, telephone, or in person, and from such inquiries new members are added.

During the first year, a governance structure was established with a senate of seven persons, now increased to nine at the apex. Standing committees have been established; bylaws have been adopted and approved by the president of the college and the board of trustees. Applications from interested persons are considered by the committee on membership; their recommendations go to the senate, whose decision on admission is final.

The basic program of ASPEC includes public lectures by its own members or by national or international leaders in various fields, and for the members and their guests, colloquies, forums, and luncheon discourses, which are supplemented by social and recreational events. Academy members who choose to do so participate with faculty and students in the academic programs of Eckerd College. In addition, ASPEC members are admitted to all the program events and activities of the college and have use of all facilities.

Some members of ASPEC are involved in projects of their own, such as writing, painting, lecturing, or consulting; one is engaged in a major project on services to the blind with foundation grants, while another is cataloguing all the jazz musical compositions produced between 1917 and 1947 with annotations and biographical information. The options available for members are numerous and extensive; selection from among them is highly individual.

On July 1, 1983, the author, Leo L. Nussbaum, a retired college president, became director of ASPEC.

Plans for the Future

Organizationally, ASPEC is an integral unit of Eckerd College, a division of the institution with its own identity, budget, governance structure, and distinctive program, yet in all its facets strongly interrelated with the other units of the college. However, declaring the academy as integral is one thing; making it so operationally is yet another matter.

Many members, when first admitted to ASPEC, tend to think of themselves as visitors or guests. Gradually they change their self-perception and take initiatives that indicate their shared territoriality, their appropriate self-esteem, and their institutional participation.

For faculty, students, administrators, and staff to accept ASPEC members also requires consistent coordination. Faculty members, from their student days to their current status in the profession, have known students as late adolescents and their colleagues generally as middle-aged. Suddenly, they have mature adults in their midst who are neither students nor faculty. How are they to be fitted into the accustomed stereotypes? Initially, they do not fit; gradually faculty cease thinking of them as adversaries and begin accepting them as colleagues. Students have responded readily to overtures from ASPEC members.

Thus, integration progresses through many small steps diplomatically executed, and through initiatives taken by many persons who understand the academy's goals — persons who venture beyond their previous experience to explore an evolving program with a vision for the future.

Eckerd College students nearly all reside on campus; in contrast, ASPEC members now are all commuters. With the construction of residences, many ASPEC members will reside on campus, not only for four years but probably for the rest of their lives.

Now on preconstruction sale are 291 residential units of College Harbor, a retirement center being constructed on the spacious waterfront campus. The retirement center (for persons age sixty-five or more), with its medical and nursing facilities, was planned and will be managed and operated by one of the nation's most experienced and most successful firms in development and management of retirement centers.

In addition to the retirement center, some 475 condominium residential units will be constructed to be occupied by members of the Academy of Senior Professionals with a minimum age of fifty-five. The composite of a conference center, club-house, auditorium, recreational facilities, and a small shopping center will be known as ASPEC Village. Together, these facilities will occupy seventy-eight acres and will adjoin buildings and facilities for the 1,100 students in the undergraduate programs of Eckerd College. Occupants will be either members of ASPEC or sustainers who, though not members, provide financial support. Three or four years hence, the total membership in ASPEC should be several hundred. Spouses of members are associate members, entitled to participate in most of the activities and events of the academy; thus, ASPEC village may have a population of 1,200 to 1,300. Other ASPEC members will continue to live within commuting distance of the campus.

Academically, College Harbor should provide a source of undergraduate internships in management, sociology, human resources, and psychology as well as a base for a great variety of research projects.

Many students will have part-time employment within ASPEC Village, thus providing them with financial aid at a location within walking distance from their residence halls.

Academy members, persons with records of high achievement in the professions and other careers, make possible an experiment combining undergraduate education with gerontology, the enthusiasm and vigor of youth with the judiciousness of maturity. The academy provides a distinctive climate for continuing intellectual and cultural stimulation, a venture enabling the generations to learn from each other, thus greatly enriching all participants.

In times past, colleges and universities did not teach the applied arts; the physical and biological sciences had to earn their places; libraries were more repositories than resources for research; feeding and entertaining students were not the proper functions of institutions of higher education. Now, connecting and engaging in the undergraduate college the experiences, intellectual acumen, initiative, creativity, and cultivated curiosity of persons who have discretionary use of their leisure time may turn out to be another pregnant idea whose time is due. ASPEC may well be a model that will be emulated in a hundred places.

References

Academy of Senior Professionals at Eckerd College. *The Academy Brochure.* St. Petersburg, Florida: Academy of Senior Professionals at Eckerd College, 1980.

Committee on Organization. *Prospectus of the Academy of Senior Professionals at Eckerd College,* St. Petersburg, Florida: Academy of Senior Professionals at Eckerd College, 1980.

Leo L. Nussbaum is director of the Academy of Senior Professionals at Eckerd College and president emeritus of Coe College, Cedar Rapids, Iowa. He has served as dean of three colleges, as a professor of psychology, and as a Fulbright lecturer to the University of Mysore, India.

.

*In view of the increasing number of mid-career and seasoned
faculty, today's challenge for American colleges and
universities is to explore innovative approaches that take
into account the interests of higher education while meeting
the needs and utilizing the talents of senior faculty.*

Responding to Institutional
Concerns and Faculty Needs

Chandra M. N. Mehrotra

The authors of the preceding chapters have laid out the problems and
challenges related to aging faculty, have presented developmental
theories and implications for faculty and administrators, have out-
lined faculty needs at different points in the academic career, have
distinguished changes that are age-related from those that are cohort-
related, have described the preretirement feelings and concerns of
professors and administrators, and have described some examples
of programs and activities that provide continued enrichment and
stimulation to senior professionals. In this chapter, I comment on
some of the issues that the authors have raised in terms of institutional concerns and faculty needs, reviewing the psychological characteristics of senior faculty and the relationship of these characteristics to performance. In addition, I discuss the role of systematic
performance appraisal in the decision-making process, and conclude
with exploration of innovative approaches that can meet faculty needs
and utilize their expertise and insights while maintaining instructional
quality.

C. M. N. Mehrotra (Ed.). *Teaching and Aging.* New Directions
for Teaching and Learning, no. 19. San Francisco: Jossey-Bass, September 1984.

Institutional Concerns

As pointed out by George and Winfield-Laird in Chapter One, the negative effects associated with aging faculty include the increased cost of higher education, reduction in administrative flexibility, limited inflow of new ideas and skills, and restricted employment opportunities for minorities and women. A close look at these negative implications indicates that these problems may be aggravated by additional factors such as the general economic situation in the United States, substantial declining enrollments in institutions of higher education, and a shift in the enrollment patterns from academic disciplines such as history, political science, and philosophy to applied fields such as engineering and computer science.

On the one hand, then, we have a large number of faculty in their forties and fifties who want to continue to work until they are at least seventy, and, on the other hand, we have a no-growth situation that makes it difficult to infuse new blood into institutions of higher education.

A related institutional concern has to do with the reduced enrollments of students in graduate programs, especially in the humanities. The fact that there are limited opportunities for recent Ph.D.s interested in teaching may further deter college graduates from undertaking doctoral study in preparation for a career in teaching. Furthermore, there is a real decline in the ability level of those who do enter graduate study (Bowen, 1981; Commission on Graduate Education, 1982). George and Winfield-Laird argue that this will be the most serious implication of an aging academic labor force, since it threatens the quality of future teaching and research efforts in academic organizations.

Thus, the challenge for American colleges and universities is that of balancing the interests of higher education (specifically, the generation of new knowledge, provision of quality education, and maintenance of the viability of academic careers for young adults) while meeting the needs of and utilizing the talents of mid-career and seasoned professors.

Faculty Needs

These institutional concerns are at least in part due to the age structure of the faculty; let us now look at the situation from the point of view of the faculty members.

In Chapter Two, Claxton and Murrell provided a detailed discussion of Erikson's and Loevinger's theories of human development, and Baldwin, in Chapter Three, presented the career development implications of faculty needs. There are other theoretical frameworks related to human needs that can be applied to faculty career development — such frameworks as provided by Maslow (1943), Alderfer (1969), and McClusky (1982). We will not describe these hierarchical theories in any detail here. It is sufficient for our purposes to draw the reader's attention to the basic concept that underlies these theories. In each case, the needs are arranged in a hierarchy of importance; one's behavior is controlled chiefly by the lowest need that is still unsatisfied. In Maslow's hierarchy, for example, the basic survival needs are at the bottom and the distinctly human ones (self-actualization or the need to realize one's potential) at the top.

Instead of postulating five types or levels of need, Alderfer suggests three basic human needs: *Existence, Relatedness,* and *Growth.* Although Alderfer's ERG theory is concerned with the same needs as Maslow's, it views the needs as operating in different ways. The ERG needs are not rigidly hierarchical. More than one of these needs can operate at the same time, and satisfaction of one need does not lead automatically to a higher need. Unlike Maslow, Alderfer suggests that satisfaction of a need may increase its intensity. An important implication of this theory is that, instead of being fulfilled, the relatedness and growth needs of senior faculty continue to become stronger, necessitating opportunities for interactions with other people and for new challenges that lead to personal growth and development.

In line with Maslow's notion of social (belongingness or love) needs and self-esteem needs and with Alderfer's relatedness needs, the research reported by Myers and Pearson in Chapter Five indicates that faculty and administrators within five years of retirement value the community where they have lived during their academic career and are thinking about contributing to the community by using professional skills and experience. Maintaining personal contacts both with the institution and the community is important to those anticipating retirement. A recent study (Kaye and Monk, 1983) confirms that retired academics are concerned about the loss of contact with their colleagues and about reduced intellectual stimulation. One approach to overcoming this problem is described by Nussbaum in Chapter Six.

Another example is provided by the Academy of Independent Scholars formed by Kenneth Boulding and Lawrence Senesh to serve retired scholars (as well as former leaders in business, labor, government, and civic organizations) who seek opportunities for continued creative work. According to a Carnegie Corporation report (1982), this academy brings together interdisciplinary groups of educators to work on problems that affect the United States and the world. Moreover, the academy held a summer institute in 1980 for high school students to discuss economic growth, energy, and the quality of life. Thus the academy acts as a catalyst for putting to use the ideas of highly experienced individuals, promoting intergenerational interaction, and meeting the social and intellectual needs of retired scholars and professionals.

Other examples of institutions that facilitate continued growth of older adults by utilizing the talent of retired executives and emeritus professors include the Academy of Lifelong Learning at the University of Delaware, the Institute for Retired Professionals at the New School in New York City, and the Education Network of Older Adults in Chicago (Buchmann, 1983).

Unlike the gratification of the social and self-esteem needs, gratifying the self-actualization need does not reduce its potency; in fact, the more chances a person has to realize his or her potential, the greater the need to self-actualize becomes. McClusky (1982) describes the hierarchy of needs in an educational context. This hierarchy is similar to that of Maslow and includes coping needs, expressive needs, contributive needs, influence needs, and the need for transcendence. Obviously, there is considerable similarity between the need to self-actualize and the need for transcendence. An important implication of these theories is that both younger and older faculty members need opportunities for growth so that they continue to realize their potential. Contrary to the common belief that faculty members stop trying new approaches to teaching after they have received tenure, teaching effectiveness seems to be maintained (McKeachie, 1983).

In view of the large individual differences among older adults (Heron and Chown, 1967), seasoned faculty members should have the freedom to choose the growth opportunities they consider most beneficial. Maslow's concept of self-actualization and Erikson's notion of generativity also imply that faculty members of all ages have a need to produce something that will outlive themselves, to leave their mark in some way (Schaie and Strother, 1968; Kimmel, 1980). The challenge for college and university administrators is that of providing an environment that will facilitate the achievement of these higher-order needs. Realization of these needs will lead not only to higher levels of job satisfaction in faculty members of all ages but also to teaching improvement and the generation of new knowledge.

A related challenge has to do with communicating the institution's expectations to the members of the faculty. If we expect less from older faculty, we will get less. If we provide them with new opportunities that utilize their expertise, they will rise to these expectations and will continue to contribute in new ways.

Faculty Characteristics

Since one of the institutional concerns deals with the issue of faculty performance, this section discusses faculty characteristics relevant to teaching. Though real declines do occur in vision, hearing, reaction time, and sensory motor functions in later life, one can compensate for some of these losses, and most of them have little impact upon academic performance (McKeachie, 1983). A recent survey of college faculty conducted by Hansen and Holden (1981) indicates that this group is a longer-lived and healthier one than is the general population. These investigators report that, from age sixty onwards, death rates for faculty are only about half those of the general population; life expectation is from twenty-five to forty percent longer. One implication of these findings may be that there is less decline in the above functions for college faculty than for the population in general. There is a popular saying in gerontology, "Use it or lose it"; thus, faculty members are able to maintain those functions that they use on a regular basis.

Probably the characteristic most relevant to teaching, research, and community service is that of verbal intelligence — the abilities, as measured by the Wechsler Adult Intelligence Scale, involving vocabulary, information, and comprehension. Recent studies indicate that these abilities are maintained beyond the age of seventy.

In addition, we do not find significant age differences in the performance of activities in a particular place of employment. Salthouse (1982) indicates that very little is presently known about how experience changes the nature of skills, but is obvious that experience leads to dramatic improvements in the efficiency and effectiveness of performance.

It follows, therefore, that many highly practiced activities may be maintained at a constant level despite age-related declines in component abilities because of the compensating effects of greater experience and because of effective use of the maintained abilities. Earlier in this chapter, we cited a study from the Center for Research on Learning and Teaching at Michigan (McKeachie, 1983) that confirms the notion that teaching effectiveness is indeed maintained by faculty members as they age. Similar findings have been reported by investigators who have examined the relationship of age and performance in other types of work (Holley and others, 1978).

Finally, learning ability does not decline significantly with advancing age, and any decline that does appear is often more related to motivation and physiological condition than to learning capacity (Birren, 1964). Indeed, many elderly individuals, especially those who are college graduates, perform well above the average of young adults on a measure of Educational Aptitude, a linear combination of the Primary Mental Abilities tests for vocabulary recognition and inductive reasoning (Schaie and Parham, 1977; Schaie and Strother, 1968). Schaie and Willis (1979) have stated "that, indeed, the fact that we can document an increasing number of individual instances of lack of individual decline on important psychological functions suggests that the average decrement observed beyond the sixties may well be pathology-related or modifiable by social interventions" (p. 130).

It has also been demonstrated (Schaie and Gribbin, 1975) that there is very little decrement in function at most ages over periods as long as fourteen years in individuals who have a complex environment and who are involved in many interpersonal contacts, while substantial decrement is noted in those living isolated lives. It follows, then, that faculty members in their forties and fifties can benefit from faculty development activities, can learn new skills, and can assume new responsibilities. The fact that such a large number of them have developed new competencies related to the use of computers in their teaching and research activities is an indication of their learning ability.

Nevertheless, those involved in working with these faculty members should remember that there are substantial differences in abilities, maintenance patterns, and willingness to assume new responsibilities. Schaie (1977/78) reminds us that in adulthood the developmental tasks (Havighurst (1972) of the individual change, and the objectives of the individual may no longer be primarily directed toward skills acquisition but toward the application of acquired skills to responsible social roles and societal tasks. The challenge for the institution, therefore, is to determine which individuals are still interested in acquiring new skills and which ones are more inclined toward the application of skills they already have.

In short, there is considerable evidence to show that (1) intellectual decline takes place later and more slowly than is generally assumed, (2) stimulating environment and interpersonal contact play an important role in enabling older adults to maintain their cognitive functioning, (3) experience and practice enable senior faculty to maintain teaching effectiveness, and (4) individual differences *within* older faculty are greater than the variance *between* age groups.

Performance Appraisal

We have mentioned several times that there exists a large range of individual differences among the older faculty. These differences are found in a number of areas, such as abilities, interests, attitudes, and motivation for continued employment. This implies that programs and activities that are suggested later in this section cannot be applied mechanically to all faculty. Instead, institutions of higher education should offer preretirement planning programs for faculty of all ages and make a variety of options regarding work and retirement available to senior faculty.

It follows that public policy should be based on age-neutral or age-irrelevant factors and that decisions regarding a person's access to a job be based on his or her ability to perform rather than on the number of years he or she has lived. This implies the need for conducting systematic evaluation of faculty performance on a regular basis and for utilizing the findings of performance appraisal with an analysis of institutional needs in making decisions about senior faculty.

The Freedom of Information Act and the 1978 amendments to the Age Discrimination in Employment Act (ADEA) also point to the critical need for conducting performance appraisal of faculty of all ages. Appraisals should be conducted on a regular basis, should aim to achieve the goals of equity and age neutrality, and should satisfy the criteria of reliability, reasonableness, and relevance. Effective performance appraisal should utilize a variety of methods, such as systematic observation of classroom teaching; review of course syllabi, research proposals, and publications; examination of students' ratings; and discussion of the faculty member's objectives and self-assessment. An excellent discussion of the various approaches to faculty evaluation is available in such sources as Kirschling (1978) and Millman (1981).

Our discussion here is confined to those elements that most strongly affect the mid-career and mature faculty. In order to make the appraisal system useful to the institutions as well as to faculty, we suggest that faculty be involved in its design and execution. In discussing faculty objectives as a part of performance appraisal, the evaluator should give attention to (1) what has been accomplished; (2) job satisfaction, skills, and work-related aspirations; and (3) developing plans, benchmarks, and expected results by which to measure future performance (Rosow and Zager, 1980). Thus, the reviewing of objectives and of self-assessment of performance provides an excellent opportunity for interaction between the faculty member and his or her supervisor. Also, as I have indicated elsewhere (Mehrotra, 1983), it is important that written evaluations be retained on a regular basis. Courts favor appraisal programs that are systematic rather than ad hoc or haphazard. Their view indicates concern for equity and for regular, recurring age-neutral appraisals.

Research in business and industry has demonstrated that it is possible to reduce errors in performance evaluation by training the appraisers. This training should not only cover the administrative aspects of the program but should also help the appraiser to understand the objectives, problems, and the behavioral aspects of performance evaluation. Since the effects of training may diminish over time, refresher courses are also necessary.

The information obtained by conducting systematic appraisal is helpful to institutions in making personnel decisions regarding salary, continued employment, and faculty development. This information is also helpful to the individual faculty members in providing them with valuable feedback regarding their effectiveness.

An example of such use of performance appraisal can be found at Hastings College of the Law at the University of California. Since about one-fourth of Hastings faculty are retired professors and judges from institutions across the country, performance appraisal plays a vital role in the decision-making process. The appraisal system is used when these potential faculty members are invited to serve as visiting professors at Hastings and is again used in deciding whether they should be invited to join the college staff. This decision is based on past accomplishments (including publications and other contributions) and on teaching effectiveness. After they join the faculty, performance appraisal is used regularly in making continuation decisions.

Hastings also provides an excellent model of the intergenerational collaboration and interaction recommended by McClusky (1978) and the 1981 White House Conference on Aging. As Barnes (1978) indicates, "It is amazing to an outsider how easy the relationship is between students and teachers so markedly different in age" (p. 355). In addition to members of the 65 Club (a group comprised of superannuated but not retired professors), the college faculty includes many other members with ages ranging from thirty to sixty and with about one-fourth of the faculty over sixty-five. These members of the 65 Club bring a wealth of experience, insights, and invaluable perspective from their work in other institutions including the United States Supreme Court and the California Supreme Court. It is no surprise that this unique faculty attracts students from all over the country.

This brief discussion of the Hastings model provides a glimpse of several innovative features: the effective use of performance appraisal, the utilization of the talent and expertise of older faculty and other professionals, and the intergenerational interaction among faculty members of different ages. Performance appraisal has also been used by community colleges that utilize the retired faculty members from other institutions of higher education. Decisions regarding continuation of these faculty are made on a year-to-year basis using the information provided by an evaluation of their teaching effectiveness.

Innovative Approaches to Utilizing Senior Faculty

In Chapter One, George and Winfield-Laird presented a number of potential interventions that could be implemented by colleges and universities to overcome problems arising from an aging academic labor force. Their discussion represents the institutional perspective. Looking at the situation from the point of view of the individuals involved, one finds that four-fifths of the workers between fifty-five and sixty-four years of age are opposed to stopping work completely (Harris and Associates, 1981). Studies of the college faculty indicate similar trends. A recent survey conducted by Hansen and Holden (1982) to study the faculty response to the change in mandatory retirement age (MRA) showed that a large number of professors had indeed decided to delay retirement. In view of improved health care, a large proportion of college faculty who are currently in their forties and fifties will be able to maintain competence and health much beyond the MRA. It is, therefore, important to explore innovative approaches that enable institutions of higher education to utilize the valuable human resources represented by senior faculty. I present some possible work options in this section.

Before describing these alternatives, however, I should reiterate that decisions regarding work and retirement should be based on the findings of systematic performance appraisal. This practice is not only defensible but will prove advantageous to the institution as well as to faculty members. It will enable institutions to make effective use of the talent and expertise of senior faculty who, in turn, will achieve higher levels of job satisfaction by participating in activities that provide them with appropriate challenges and opportunities. The following subsections describe some of these activities.

Phased Retirement. Since college faculty maintain better health than their counterparts in other professions and since they prefer to keep working beyond the retirement age and are able to maintain teaching effectiveness, we should explore the option of gradually decreasing their hours and responsibilities over a period of several years. This option provides opportunities for junior faculty and opens up new positions for young adults interested in an academic career. In a study conducted for the American Management Association by Robert Jud (Buchmann, 1983), researchers found that higher-paid managers were most likely to choose to continue to work on a reduced schedule and at less intensity. Variations on the phased retirement theme include rehearsal retirement and job reassignments. Both the favorable experience with these approaches in business and industry and the interest of older faculty in reduced work hours point to the need for increased use of these options in colleges and universities.

In Chapter Three, Baldwin has suggested that the unique talents of selected senior faculty can be utilized by giving them fresh assignments — assignments that provide them with new challenges and opportunities and enable the institution to achieve its goals. Examples of such assignments include working in the development office to initiate new proposals, contacting alumni for fund raising and other purposes, working with junior faculty to explore new areas for research, reviewing grant applications prepared by others, teaching introductory courses, performing interdisciplinary teaching, sharing expertise with the community at large, and assisting the admissions staff in making contacts with prospective students. This is not a comprehensive list of possible fresh assignments for mature faculty, but it is given here to indicate the large variety of possibilities from which the selection can be made depending upon the individual's background and interests and the institutional needs. On the basis of our favorable experience at St. Scholastica with some of these approaches, we can recommend them to other institutions. We are also aware of the phased retirement program at the University of San Diego, designed to provide the faculty with an opportunity "to reduce their regular appointments to pursue personal or professional lives in gainful part-time employment" (University of San Diego, 1980, p. 7). This cost-effective approach can lead to a great degree of job satisfaction for the participants while enabling the institution to continue to draw upon their wisdom, judgment, commitment, and experience.

These job reassignment possibilities should not be confined to what is available within the college or university. Businesses and other organizations in the community also provide excellent opportunities for utlizing the expertise of senior faculty. Research conducted by Hansen and Holden (1981) suggests the importance of institutional affiliation in obtaining consulting contracts, speaking engagements, and other such opportunities that might not be forthcoming in retirement. These investigators conclude that a continuing faculty appointment is, therefore, necessary to assure involvement in other professional activities.

Developing such ties between colleges and external agencies will be helpful to both and will open new doors for younger faculty and students as well. Establishing such "service bureaus" in the institutions of higher education will also complement students' cognitive learning in the classroom with experiential learning in community agencies.

Part-Time Employment. While phased retirement implies gradual decrease in number of hours and in responsibilities, part-time employment may be continued indefinitely. This approach allows the faculty to work less than the prevailing standard number of hours. Due to varying definitions of part-time work, data on the number of faculty working part-time are inexact. However, institutions of higher education do employ a large number of part-time faculty, and this number has continued to increase (Leslie, 1978). Generally, the requirements of teaching experience, specific competencies, and the terminal degree in one's discipline have restricted the supply of part-time faculty, especially in smaller communities. But these attributes are not lacking in the older faculty, a subgroup with growing interest in part-time employment. The economic advantages that accrue to employers of part-time faculty in general may be increased further when these faculty are drawn from senior members. Copperman and Keast (1983) list a number of advantages of employing older workers on a part-time basis. In the case of older faculty these advantages include: (1) skills and competencies that match institutional needs; (2) lower turnover rates than those of younger part-time faculty; (3) self-discipline and a mature approach to job responsibilities; (4) conscientiousness and reliability as employees; (5) job stability; and (6) experience and good work habits, which reduce the need for supervision or training and thus reduce costs of the institution.

In light of the advantages listed above, a number of colleges and universities have developed programs of part-time employment for senior faculty. One such program (referred to in the preceding section) is offered by the University of San Diego. This program allows participants "to phase down the reduction in time-base gradually, or initially to reduce an appointment at a certain fraction and remain at that fraction until full retirement" (University of San Diego, 1980, p. 9). Since interest in part-time work is significantly related to the individual's perception that this is an available alternative, there is a clear need to publicize the availability of this option. This approach is likely to result in potential retirees giving serious consideration to part-time work as a realistic alternative to full-time work followed by abrupt retirement.

It should, however, be pointed out that findings from faculty evaluations and from institutional need analyses should be used in making a decision regarding which faculty members are offered a part-time contract.

As in the case of phased retirement, a program of part-time employment contributes toward the university's mission of academic excellence by allowing it to retain the services and contributions of senior faculty, while enabling the participants to continue the exercise of their profession and to build additional security for the future. This program also assists in diversifying the institution's work force by releasing positions and funds that can be used for new appointments.

College planning to institute a program of part-time employment also needs to develop detailed analyses of the impact of such employment on the pension benefits of mature employees, an important factor used by such employees in their decisions concerning part-time work. Similar analyses also need to be done in the case of faculty members selecting the option of phased retirement. Finally, a comparative analysis should be conducted to assess the costs and benefits of these approaches as compared to other options (see Chapter One), including the early retirement incentive approach that has been implemented by some institutions (Patton, 1978; Hansen and Holden, 1981).

Contract Employment. The experience of business and industry indicates that the employment of retired faculty as independent contractors offers interesting opportunities. Since many of the retired faculty already receive their basic income from pension benefits, they may be particularly willing to consider contracts for specific tasks that they can do at their convenience. This approach may provide them with an opportunity to maintain their participation in the labor force while continuing to enjoy their leisure activities.

This option deserves special attention in view of the rapid advances of technology in education. Cost reductions will make microcomputers accessible to a large segment of our population, and the need for instructional software will continue to grow. Preparing quality software that can be used for computer-assisted instruction involves collaboration between computer programmers and specialists in the content area. Retired faculty with valuable teaching experience can make important contributions in developing and reviewing computer software for instructional purposes. This approach requires no financial investment on their part and has the advantage of drawing upon their wealth of accumulated experience and insights. Increased access to microcomputers will also enable the retired faculty to do the bulk of their contract work at home. Activities involved in software development include such tasks as designing and writing instructional materials, reviewing software prepared by others, and conducting pilot runs and data analysis and interpretation.

Editing books, monographs, and journals on a contract basis offers another possibility for employment. As we have discussed in an earlier section of this chapter, senior faculty maintain verbal intelligence much beyond the traditional retirement age. Indeed, the average age of the Sixty-Five Club members at Hastings is seventy-three; the oldest member is eighty-three. Editorial work provides an excellent opportunity for utilizing verbal abilities, and it meets the faculty member's need to contribute. Other related possibilities include reviewing scripts that instructors plan to use in videotapes for distant learners, reviewing grant proposals for funding agencies, and writing test items for national examinations.

In short, we suggest the value of the contract employment option in meeting the needs of retired faculty members who are unable to participate in the other programs described here. This approach provides them with flexibility in terms of working hours, allows them to be selective in the amount and type of work that they undertake, enables them to continue using their abilities, and permits them to make useful contributions as long as they are able to do so. That they can do a large portion of the work at home and still maintain some contact with the academic world makes this approach even more attractive.

Conclusion

We have suggested some alternatives that would extend the working life of senior faculty and would facilitate the transition from full-time work to complete retirement. We have also pointed out that senior faculty constitute a very diverse group of individuals; decisions for the individual faculty member cannot be made on the basis of age-group norms. Instead, the decisions should be based on the findings of systematic performance appraisal that provides objective evidence on individuals' teaching effectiveness and on their ability to contribute in other ways toward the mission of the institution. Such an approach to decision making would enable colleges and universities to make optimum use of available talent regardless of age group. This age-neutral policy would also lead to the development of a community of generations within the participating institutions, which will benefit from the unique contributions by members of all ages. Such intergenerational collaboration will not only meet important social needs of its members but will also give them an opportunity to learn from one another.

What we propose may seem idealistic, but we feel that the ideal

96

of conserving valuable human resources and honoring people's right to work is worth striving for. The costs of making this proposal a reality may be high and the development of new policies and their implementations may involve a considerable amount of work, but the benefits of treating human beings with dignity and respect, giving them the freedom to make choices, and utilizing their knowledge, wisdom, and insights in educational endeavors are much greater than the material costs.

References

Alderfer, C. P. "A New Theory of Human Needs." *Organizational Behavior and Human Performance,* 1969, *4,* 142–175.
Barnes, T. G. *Hastings College of the Law: The First Century.* San Francisco: Hastings College of the Law Press, 1978.
Birren, J. E. *The Psychology of Aging.* Englewood Cliffs, N.J.: Prentice-Hall, 1964.
Bowen, W. G. *Graduate Education in the Arts and Sciences: Prospects for the Future.* Princeton, N.J.: Princeton University, 1981.
Buchmann, A. M. "Maximizing Postretirement Labor Market Opportunities." In H. A. Parnes (Ed.), *Policy Issues in Work and Retirement.* Kalamazoo: Upjohn Institute, 1983.
Carnegie Corporation of New York. *The List of Grants 1982.* New York: Carnegie Corporation of New York, 1982.
Commission on Graduate Education. "Report of the Commission on Graduate Education." *University of Chicago Record,* 1982, *16* (2), entire volume.
Copperman, L. F., and Keast, F. D. *Adjusting to an Older Work Force.* New York: Van Nostrand Reinhold, 1983.
Hansen, W. L., and Holden, K. C. "Major Results of the Wisconsin Study for the Department of Labor." Unpublished manuscript, University of Wisconsin, Madison, 1981.
Hansen, W. L., and Holden, K. C. "Report of 1980 Study and 1982 Follow-up Survey on Academic Retirement." Unpublished manuscript, University of Wisconsin, Madison, 1982.
Harris, L., and Associates. *Aging in the Eighties: America in Transition.* Washington, D.C.: National Council on Aging, 1981.
Havighurst, R. J. *Developmental Tasks and Education.* (3rd ed.) New York: David McKay, 1972.
Heron, A., and Chown, S. *Age and Function.* London: Churchill, 1967.
Holley, W. H., Field, H. S., and Holley, B. B. "Age and Reactions to Jobs: An Empirical Study of Paraprofessional Workers." *Aging and Work,* 1978, *1,* 33–40.
Kaye, L., and Monk, A. "Leaving the Ivory Tower: Problems and Rewards of the Retired Academic." Paper presented at the 36th annual scientific meeting of the Gerontological Society of America, San Francisco, November 1983.
Kimmel, D. C. *Adulthood and Aging.* (2nd ed.) New York: Wiley, 1980.
Kirschling, W. C. (Ed.). *Evaluating Faculty Performance and Vitality.* New Directions for Institutional Research, no. 20. San Francisco: Jossey-Bass, 1978.
Leslie, D. W. *Employing Part-Time Faculty.* New Directions for Institutional Research, no. 18. San Francisco: Jossey-Bass, 1978.
Maslow, A. H. "A Theory of Human Motivation." *Psychological Review,* 1943, *50,* 370–396.
McClusky, H. Y. "The Community of Generations: A Goal and a Context for the Education of Persons in the Later Years." In R. M. Sharron and D. B. Lumsden (Eds.), *Introduction to Educational Gerontology.* Washington, D.C.: Hemisphere, 1978.

97

McClusky, H. Y. "Education for Older Adults." In C. Eisdorfer (Ed.), *Annual Review of Gerontology and Geriatrics.* Vol. 3. New York: Springer, 1982.
McKeachie, W. J. "Faculty as a Renewable Resource." In R. T. Blackburn and R. Baldwin (Eds.), *College Faculty: Versatile Resources in a Period of Constraint.* New Directions for Institutional Research, no. 39. San Francisco: Jossey-Bass, 1983.
Mehrotra, C. "Appraising the Performance of Older Workers." Paper presented at the NATO-Sponsored Symposium on Aging and Technological Advances, University of Southern California, Los Angeles, 1983.
Millman, J. (Ed.). *Handbook of Teacher Evaluation.* Beverly Hills: Sage, 1981.
Patton, C. V. "Mid-Career Change and Early Retirement." In W. R. Kirschling (Ed.), *Evaluating Faculty Performance and Vitality.* New Directions for Institutional Research, no. 20. San Francisco: Jossey-Bass, 1978.
Rosow, M., and Zager, R. *The Future of Older Workers in America: New Options for an Extended Work Life.* Scarsdale, N.Y.: Work in America Institute, 1980.
Salthouse, T. A. *Adult Cognition: An Experimental Psychology of Human Aging.* New York: Springer-Verlag, 1982.
Schaie, K. W. "Toward a Stage Theory of Adult Cognitive Development." *Journal of Aging and Human Development,* 1977/78, *8,* 129–138.
Schaie, K. W., and Strother, C. R. "The Cross-Sequential Study of Age Changes in Cognitive Behavior." *Psychological Bulletin,* 1968, *70,* 671–680.
Schaie, K. W., and Gribbin, K. *The Impact of Environmental Complexity upon Adult Cognitive Development.* Paper presented at the biennial meeting of the International Society for the Study of Behavioral Development, Guilford, England, 1975.
Schaie, K. W., and Parham, I. A. "Cohort-Sequential Analysis of Adult Intellectual Development." *Developmental Psychology,* 1977, *13,* 649–653.
Schaie, K. W., and Willis, S. L. "Life-Span Development: Implications for Education." In L. S. Shulman (Ed.), *Review of Research in Education.* Vol. 6. Itasca, Ill.: Peacock, 1979.
University of San Diego. *The University of San Diego Phased Retirement Program.* Unpublished report, San Diego, Calif.: University of San Diego, 1980.

Chandra M. N. Mehrotra is a professor of psychology and associate dean for graduate studies at the College of St. Scholastica. His research and intellectual interests include the education and employment of older adults.

Index

13; flexibility in, 13-14; in human development business, 42; inflow of skills and ideas for, 14; institutional concerns in, 83-97; as no-growth, 9-10; quality of, and aging faculty, 5-27; shared perceptions of mission for, 43

Hodgkinson, H. L., 46, 56, 57, 58-59, 64

Holden, K. C., 87, 91, 92-93, 94, 96

Holley, B. B., 96

Holley, W. H., 88, 96

I

Indentity stage, in faculty development, 31, 32, 43

Individualistic level, in faculty development, 35

Institute for Retired Professionals, 86

Institutional service, by senior faculty, 51-52

Integrated stage, in faculty development, 36

Integrity stage, in faculty development, 32, 33

Intimacy stage, in faculty development, 31-33

J

Jenny, H. H., 16, 26

Jud, R., 92

K

Kaye, L., 85, 96

Keast, F. D., 93, 96

Kell, D., 16, 26

Keller, G., 41, 42, 44

Kimmel, D. C., 50, 56, 86, 96

Kimmel, D. D., 67, 74

Kirschling, W. C., 89, 96

Knefelkamp, L, 33, 44

Knepper, P. R., 6, 12, 26

Kohlberg, L., 42, 44

L

Ladd, E. C., 46, 56

Lawrence, J. H., 2, 57-65

Leadership, and developmental theory, 41-43

Legislation, on retirement age, 11

Leslie, D. W., 93, 96

Levinson, D. J., 48, 56, 58, 64

Lipset, S. M., 46, 56

Loevinger, J., 2, 30, 33-36, 42, 43, 44, 85

M

McCain, B. E., 62, 64

McClusky, H. Y., 85, 86, 90, 96

McDowell, J. M., 20, 25

McKeachie, W. J., 53, 54, 56, 60, 64, 86, 87, 97

Maddox, G., 11, 26

Mann, W. R., 23, 26

Maslow, A. H., 85, 86, 97

Mehrotra, C. M. N., 1-3, 83-97

Mentoring, by senior faculty, 50, 52

Merton, R. K., 14, 26

Michigan, University of, faculty career study at, 62

Millman, J., 89, 97

Minorities, effects of aging on, 14

Monk, A., 85, 96

Moore, W. L., 62, 64

Murrell, P. H., 2, 29-44, 50, 85

Myers, B. J., 2, 67-74, 85

N

Naisbitt, J., 42-43, 44

National Science Foundation, 6, 7, 8, 9, 10, 12, 15, 24, 26

New School, Institute for Retired Professionals at, 86

Nussbaum, L. L., 2, 75-82

O

O'Reilly, C., 64

Ory, J. C., 64

P

Palmer, F. H., 78

Parham, I. A., 88, 97

Parker, C. A., 44

Parsons, T., 61, 64

Patton, C. V., 16, 26, 94, 97

Pearson, R. E., 2, 67-74, 85

Pelz, D. C., 46, 56, 59, 64

Performance appraisal, for senior faculty, 89-91